The Book of Job

Selected Books in the
SkyLight Illuminations Series

The Book of Job

Annotated & Explained

Translation & Annotation by Donald Kraus

Foreword by Dr. Marc Brettler

For People of All Faiths, All Backgrounds

JEWISH LIGHTS Publishing
Woodstock, Vermont

Walking Together, Finding the Way ®
SKYLIGHT PATHS®
PUBLISHING
Woodstock, Vermont

The Book of Job: Annotated & Explained

2012 Quality Paperback Edition, First Printing
Translation, annotation, and introductory material © 2012 by Donald Kraus
Foreword © 2012 by Marc Brettler

Library of Congress Cataloging-in-Publication Data

Bible. O.T. Job. English. Kraus. 2012.
  The book of Job annotated & explained / translation and annotation by Donald Kraus ;
foreword by Marc Brettler.
    p. cm. — (Walking together, finding the way) (Skylight illuminations)
  Includes bibliographical references.
  ISBN 978-1-59473-389-5 (pbk.)
  1. Bible. O.T. Job.—Commentaries. I. Kraus, Donald. II. Title. III. Title: Book of Job
annotated and explained.
  BS1413.K73 2012
  223'.1077—dc23
                        2012018006

10 9 8 7 6 5 4 3 2 1

Manufactured in the United States of America

Cover Design: Walter C. Bumford III, Stockton, Massachusetts, and Gloria Todt
Cover Art: © rolffimages/Fotolia.com

SkyLight Paths Publishing is creating a place where people of different spiritual
traditions come together for challenge and inspiration, a place where we can help
each other understand the mystery that lies at the heart of our existence.

SkyLight Paths sees both believers and seekers as a community that increasingly
transcends traditional boundaries of religion and denomination—people wanting
to learn from each other, *walking together, finding the way*.

SkyLight Paths, "Walking Together, Finding the Way" and colophon are trademarks of
LongHill Partners, Inc., registered in the U.S. Patent and Trademark Office.

Walking Together, Finding the Way®

Published by SkyLight Paths® Publishing and Jewish Lights Publishing
Divisions of LongHill Partners, Inc.
Sunset Farm Offices, Route 4, P.O. Box 237
Woodstock, VT 05091
Tel: (802) 457-4000   Fax: (802) 457-4004
www.skylightpaths.com   www.jewishlights.com

Contents ☐

Foreword ☐

Job's name in Hebrew may be aptly translated as "Where is the (heavenly) father?" and no other biblical book deals so powerfully with the problem of the suffering of the righteous individual in a theistic world. The majority of the book, composed of about thirty-nine of the most difficult but beautiful chapters of Hebrew poetry of the Bible, is structured in dialogue form: dialogues between Job and his three friends; responses to Job by the mysterious Elihu; and two concluding dialogues between Job and God, where, quite surprisingly, Job has the last word. Yet these are not dialogues in the sense that we are familiar with; Job does not respond to the content of his friends' speeches, nor do God and Job address each other's claims in a straightforward way. Perhaps the poet of Job means to suggest that there is no simple, straightforward answer to the profound questions that the book raises.

The majestic poetry is surrounded by a two-chapter prose introduction and a brief, eleven-verse conclusion (42:7–17). The prose presents a simple but disturbing theology: All of Job's tribulations are the result of God talking too much. Twice God says to the Provoker (or Adversary; Hebrew *ha-satan*), a member of the divine council, "Have you laid heart to my servant Job? He has no equal in the world, downright upright, holding me in awe, turning from evil" (1:8, 2:3). This conversation provokes the Adversary, who asks and gains permission to harm Job's property and family, and eventually Job himself. In the final chapter Job is restored; his property is doubled, and a "new" set of children, including three most beautiful daughters, are born to him. Indeed, a very loose translation of the book's last two verses would be: "And Job lived happily ever after." Indeed. This prose suggests that there may be "blips" in the system of divine retribution, but the person who is patient will ultimately be rewarded properly in this world. These blips are significant—the theology here is not that the righteous always prosper and the wicked are always punished, but that this is ultimately the case. And the exceptions have reasons: God's heavenly court is run better than its human counterpart, but is not run perfectly.

The book of Job is considered, like Proverbs and Ecclesiastes, a wisdom book, the product of a group of ancient Israelite sages. Yet the world goes awry when God does not listen to wisdom advice such as Proverbs 17:28, "Even fools who keep silent are considered wise; when they close their lips, they are deemed intelligent." After all, the text suggests that had God not engaged the Provoker, showing off how righteous God's "servant" Job was, none of these catastrophes would have befallen him.

The poetical center will not have any of this simple argument. Job and his friends present certain main arguments. Job insists that the righteous do suffer and that God abuses God's great power. The friends argue the opposite—only the wicked suffer, and God uses the divine power beneficently. (It is quite striking that no one in the book argues that God is not powerful and in control of the world.) After three cycles of speeches, where they each adduce their personal experiences and perceptions, they are all worn out, and we expect God to respond to Job's insistent demand: "Let the Mighty One answer! Let God issue the indictment, this opposing counsel!" (31:35). But instead we get Elihu.

Elihu presents significant interpretive problems, and many modern biblical scholars excise his speeches, claiming they are secondary. He can't shut up, is very wordy, and presents himself as full of gas: "For I am full of words; the wind within me distresses me" (32:18, author's translation). To make matters worse, the following speeches of God from the storm pick up on the vocabulary and ideas that Elihu expresses. Does Elihu thus foreshadow God or undermine God's speeches?

The language of the divine speeches is exquisite, and much more clear than the very difficult poetry elsewhere in the book. They are among the most beautiful in the Bible, but they never directly address Job's situation.

The first, in chapters 38–39, is composed of tens of rhetorical questions that focus on God's power. They thus address a shared premise of Job and his friends—that God is powerful—but do not clearly note whether this power is always used for good or not, the issue that Job and his friends debated. The second speech (40:6–41:26) is even more puzzling—its main focus is two creatures: Behemoth, a mythologized hippopotamus, and Leviathan, a mythologized crocodile. How do they relate to the main themes of the book? Does God indeed answer Job's questions through these questions and beasts—and if so, what does this answer mean?—or is God merely interested in bullying Job into submission? Scholars are deeply divided over these issues.

Perhaps Job's final words may provide some insight into the book and its ultimate meaning. But here, too, we run into an interpretive difficulty. Is Job capitulating, as suggested in most translations, including the NRSV's: "Therefore I despise myself, and repent in dust and ashes" (42:6), or has, for example, contemporary scholar and translator Stephen Mitchell properly captured the nuance of the Hebrew: "Therefore I will be quiet, comforted that I am dust"?

Perhaps the material in Job has been organized to suggest that there is no easy, obvious answer to life's most difficult questions, and this is what has made Job such a popular book. Professional Bible scholars and others, such as the ancient Greek work "The Testament of Job," William Blake in his remarkable drawings, and Archibald MacLeish in his play *JB*, have attempted to offer compelling interpretations. No one has yet succeeded, but the book, through its engaging style and important message, continues to help generation after generation address the "simple" question asked in Jeremiah 12:1, "Why does the way of the guilty prosper?" Job also shows that even though recent times may be the first to have evoked very large-scale human killing, we must remember the life of every single human individual, for that is the level on which Job offers its powerful, though ambiguous, message.

Dr. Marc Brettler,
Brandeis University

Introduction ☐

The book of Job, a theological and spiritual masterpiece as well as a classic of world literature, is a poetical expression of the human effort to understand why we suffer. Job, a righteous and innocent man, becomes the victim of a plot between God and a heavenly being who tests human integrity—a plot that, as it develops, becomes little more than a cruel joke. As a result, Job loses everything he has, even his children, and finally his health; he thereby becomes an exemplar of undeserved suffering. Throughout most of the book he sits despairing among the ashes of his former life, visited by no one but his "comforters," who only make things worse by trying to persuade him that his misfortune must make sense. That is why the book of Job is so compelling in our own day. More than any other biblical text, Job wrestles with the difficulties of the human condition, the inexplicable nature of the good or evil that can befall anyone, and the inevitable question, "Why?"

After a brief, even perfunctory, opening to set the scene and create the situation, the unknown poet who created this literary classic unleashes the power of expressive language to give shape to humanity's deepest sorrows. In chapter upon chapter, with explosive imagery, dismissing the feeble, petulant, moralizing arguments from his friends, Job curses his conception and birth, his suffering, his friends for blaming him for his sorrow—he demands answers from them and, ultimately, justice from God. He describes, and perhaps mourns, the difficulty of finding wisdom in the world we know. Finally, except for a long interruption from the character Elihu (which may have been added later by someone other than the original author), Job, by the power of his speech and his unanswerable questions, silences the friends and sits silently himself.

God does then speak to Job—but does not answer Job's questions or even allude to Job's accusations. God provides no explanation at all. Instead, in poetry at least equal to the passion of Job's outbursts, God describes a universe so deeply mysterious and so far beyond human comprehension that Job could not possibly understand an answer even if it were given to him. The God of these speeches thunders profoundly and sarcastically hurls questions back at Job's questions, moving the entire debate onto another level—not "Why did this happen? What did I do to deserve this?" but "What kind of a world is this? Does it even have a meaning that I can understand?"

For those who believe in God, the questions that Job raises (including the book's refusal to answer any questions) can be both a connection with and a separation from the divine realm. Meaning and existence seem split apart, and that split calls into question not only God's goodness but also the rational expectation that God's creation will ultimately make sense.

For those who do not believe in God, Job's questions are the ultimate challenge both to the universe and to our unbelief. They challenge the universe by laying bare the fact of meaningless existence, and they test our lack of belief because the very terms of the challenge presume a meaning these questions then deny. It does no good to scream out for fairness in a world where the words "fair" and "foul" may have no meaning, or to cry out for justice when there is no being with the power or authority to establish a standard of right or wrong. And it provides no satisfaction to deny God's existence and then to be furiously angry with God for not existing.

The book of Job, thus, is the kind of masterpiece that leaves us with discontent rather than contentment and with more questions than answers. For many present-day readers, it is also a difficult book to read and appreciate. There are several reasons for this, and so it is important to begin with some examination of what the book of Job is, why it may be difficult, and how we can prepare to overcome the barriers that it puts in our way.

What Is the Book of Job?

In the Hebrew Bible, Job is included in a section known as "the Writings" (Hebrew *Ketuvim*), the third part of the Bible (the first part, Genesis through Deuteronomy, is the *Torah* or "Teaching," and the second, *Nevi'im* or "Prophets," includes not only what modern translations treat as the prophets, such as Isaiah and Jeremiah, but also the historical narratives contained in Joshua, Judges, Samuel, and Kings). The Writings are a very diverse group, including (among other books) Chronicles, Daniel, Psalms, Proverbs, and Ecclesiastes. Placing Job in this mixed assortment does not, unfortunately, give us much help in deciding what kind of literature it is. It is generally grouped with Proverbs and Ecclesiastes in the category of "wisdom" literature, and that can help us in determining some of its possible aims (see below). But there is nothing else in the Bible quite like Job, and therefore it is necessary to look outside the collection of biblical literature to make a decision about how we will approach the book.

Except for brief narratives at the beginning and the end of the book, Job is entirely made up of speeches. One character speaks, another responds, and so on through a bit more than thirty-eight chapters. It is natural, therefore, to approach Job as a play. If it is a play, however, it is a rather unsatisfactory one because it lacks dramatic action. In the section of speeches, no one does anything; in fact, hardly anyone even moves. Lack of action is only part of the difficulty; there is also no character development. The argument moves from issue to issue, but none of the speakers seems to change in any way. Drama, in fact, is entirely confined to argument.

A better analogy for Job is the ancient literary form known as the diatribe. In our language, "diatribe" usually means an attack or a denunciation. In the ancient Near East, however, as well as in the classical world of Greece and Rome, "diatribe" meant a discourse or an argument among various participants. It served as one of the means by which a philosophical examination of an issue would be presented and took the form of a dialogue between two or more speakers, one of whom would be the author's mouthpiece, and the other or others the proponents of views that the author was determined to refute. Job seems to be a writing of this type. That is why the presentation of the situation in the opening chapters is there mostly to provide the basis for the dueling speeches that follow, and the speeches serve as an explication of alternative ways of understanding (or failing to understand) the problem of human suffering. The friends offer conventional understandings of the meaning of suffering, and Job rejects these. Thus the issue is argued out, in a form that, as it came into use around the Mediterranean world, may have been the foundation of the dialogues of Plato.

Being aware of the type of literature that the book of Job represents will save us from having expectations that it was not designed to meet. It is not a realistic narrative, and is not meant to persuade the reader that the events in it actually took place (see more on this below). It does not show any psychological character development such as we would see in a Greek tragedy, nor does it narrate exciting events (other than the disasters in the opening scenes) in the manner of the Homeric epics. Instead, it focuses exclusively on the presentation of clashing viewpoints.

The Structure of the Book of Job

The book of Job has a discernible structure.

> The prose framework: opening (chapters 1–2)
> Job's curse (chapter 3)
> The first dialogue cycle (chapters 4–14)
>> Eliphaz's first speech (chapters 4–5)
>> Job's reply (chapters 6–7)
>> Bildad's first speech (chapter 8)
>> Job's reply (chapters 9–10)
>> Zophar's first speech (chapter 11)
>> Job's reply (chapters 12–14)
> The second dialogue cycle (chapters 15–21)
>> Eliphaz's second speech (chapter 15)

Job's reply (chapters 16–17)
Bildad's second speech (chapter 18)
Job's reply (chapter 19)
Zophar's second speech (chapter 20)
Job's reply (chapter 21)
The third dialogue cycle (chapters 22–28)
Eliphaz's third speech (chapter 22)
Job's reply (chapters 23–24)
Bildad's third speech (chapter 25)
Job's reply (chapter 26)
Job maintains his integrity and explains the dire fate of the
wicked (chapter 27)
Job's interlude on wisdom (chapter 28)
Job's final speeches (chapters 29–31)
Job describes his happiness in his former life (chapter 29)
Job mourns his present misery (chapter 30)
Job reasserts his righteousness and the curses that should
befall him if he sins (chapter 31)
The Elihu explosion (chapters 32–37)
The answer of God from the storm (chapters 38–41)
Job's final reply (chapter 42, verses 1–6)
The prose framework: closing (chapter 42, verses 7–17)

When and Where Was Job Written?

Job is "set" in what seems to be the time of the patriarchs, a time when there were owners of large herds and agricultural estates—perhaps around 2000 BCE or so—and when human life was believed to be considerably longer than the seventy or so years in the normal span (Job, already an adult with grown children, lives 140 years after the events and speeches in the book). So the story looks back to an idealized but indefinite past. Could it have been written during the time in which it is set? Almost certainly not. Job's language and its approach to the problem of the suffering of the innocent indicate that it was likely written much later, during the Persian period, which lasted roughly from the mid-530s BCE to the mid-330s BCE—from the time beginning when Cyrus of Persia allowed the return of the exiled Israelites to their land to the time of the conquests of Alexander, and the Hellenization of the Mediterranean world, in the late fourth century BCE. The language of Job contains words borrowed from other, related languages (which is one of the reasons it is difficult to interpret) and seems to deal with ideas that were prevalent in the wider world of the ancient Near East during that time. But any attempt to specify a date for the writing of Job is guesswork and can only be approximate.

As with the date of composition, so the place where Job was written is unknown and probably unknowable. The book sets its narrative outside of Israel, in the land of Uz, and though it is written in Hebrew, some of the characters have Hebrew names (see commentary), and the God of the book is clearly identified with the God found in the rest of the Hebrew Bible—the creator, the source of righteousness, the epitome of strength, and so on—it is not concerned with many of the themes and events of the central biblical texts. It is at least possible that the author lived outside Israel or had spent time elsewhere, but nothing is known of the writer's identity and the text gives no clues.

What Is the Relationship between Job and Other "Wisdom" Writings in the Hebrew Bible?

The wisdom writings of the Bible—Job, Proverbs, and Ecclesiastes, plus some of the psalms, such as Psalm 119—stand in a tradition of literature that is found elsewhere in the ancient Near East. In the Bible, the wisdom writings have certain common features, such as their lack of emphasis on God's covenant with Israel, the Temple, and the Exodus, for instance, and, in the case of Proverbs, a countervailing weight on the importance of right behavior for the good life. Ecclesiastes and Job, unlike Proverbs, deny any connection between right behavior and prosperity or honor.

As contemporary readers, we must remind ourselves that at the time these books were written, there was no belief in an afterlife in which the injustices of the world would be put to rights. Ancient Israelite religion had no heaven to which human beings would be admitted; heaven was the dwelling place of God and of God's assistants, the "sons of God" or heavenly beings who were charged with carrying out God's will. But heaven was not a realm in which human beings, or their souls or resurrected bodies, would ever live. The only "afterlife" in the early biblical texts is a shadowy place known as *Sheol*, which resembles more closely the Greek idea of Hades, the abode of the dead. It is significant that in both Hades and *Sheol*, the inhabitants are regarded as "dead." They can speak under certain circumstances (usually occult or forbidden ones), and they have some sort of wraithlike existence, but they are not really alive. The inhabitants of *Sheol*, among other things, cannot praise God. There is no such thing as an "immortal soul" in early biblical literature—nothing about a human being is immortal, because the only immortal being is God.

This conviction—that when we are dead, we are dead, with no opportunity for further redress either of our goodness that went unrewarded or of our wickedness that went unpunished—lies at the heart of the arguments in the main part of the book of Job. It throws the entire burden of "virtue rewarded, vice punished" on what happens during a person's human life. This is the reason for the urgency of the arguments and for the position of the book of Proverbs that virtue will be rewarded with happiness, prosperity, and honor.

For us today, this view seems naïve in the extreme, but that is probably a superficial reading of the wisdom teaching in Proverbs. It understands that all other things being equal, a life of temperance, moderation, care for others, and uprightness of life will result in better health, better relationships with others, and a happier existence. Of course, in life all other things never are equal, and those who live ethically can end up in dire situations through no fault of their own. Still, this form of wisdom holds that the virtuous would still be better off than if they had lived a life of irresponsibility and dissipation.

Furthermore, whether life is fair or not, if we are wise we will live *as if* the reward of virtue is God's blessing on us. This is partly because we need to keep "in training" with our behavior. Just as scientists maintain that "chance favors the prepared mind," meaning that we can take advantage of a lucky break only if we recognize it when it comes, so for life as a whole, we can act ethically in difficult situations only if we have practiced acting ethically in general. It is also because, in the scheme of thought represented by the book of Proverbs, we honor our commitment to God by our right actions, whatever the consequences might be.

The Argument in the Book of Job

How does the book of Job hold together? One way to understand it is as follows. The prose framework describing Job's downfall and final restitution, with its simple scheme of virtue and reward, represents how we wish the universe would work and how it should exemplify God's justice. Job's anger—and ours, in the case of our own suffering—when virtue is not in fact rewarded is witness to our sense that the universe *should* play fair, whether it actually does so or not. The demand for fairness is itself an indication: it speaks to our faith that something like fairness in fact exists and is a standard that can be appealed to.

But the book of Job does not present this argument in a straightforward fashion, and that is a part of its artistry. The opening story, with its cartoonish characters—the pious Job, the shallow and boastful God, and the devious Adversary or Provoker—is only the first of a series of viewpoints to which we as readers are invited to subscribe, only to have the ground pulled out from under us. Job's curse in chapter 3, in which he damns not only the day he was born but also the night on which he was conceived, leads to the absurd conclusion that he would have been better off if he had never existed. In what sense anyone can be said to be "better off" if there is no person there to experience this "better" state is left unsaid.

Then come the arguments of the friends. Repetitively, monotonously, they ring the variations on their favorite themes: God does indeed reward the pious and punish the wicked. Maybe not right away, and maybe not in any way that you can see, but rest assured the wicked do not ultimately triumph, and the righteous do. And along with that argument comes the corollary: If you are suffering—and this goes for Job and for the members of his family—you must have done something wrong. Maybe it's not obvious, and maybe you don't even know what it is you've done wrong, but if God sends this suffering, then you must deserve it somehow.

Job's responses to these linked assertions basically amount to "You think so? Look around you!" Can you honestly say, Job asks over and over, that the wicked are invariably brought to justice and the righteous always triumph? If you'll only pay attention to reality, you'll see case after case in which wicked people live full lives, surrounded by family and friends, enjoying their ill-gotten gains, and when they finally die, they are accompanied to their graves by crowds of mourners and well-wishers. And as for the triumph of the righteous, once again all that is needed is a little dose of reality. Plenty of people die alone, in poverty, having never experienced all the joys of life, even though they have lived upright and moral lives. They have been as virtuous as you could wish, and they have gotten nothing for it. Job also describes his own life: his charitable deeds, his piety, his rendering of judgments in the civic life of his town, the respect in which all around him would hold him, and the deference that they would pay him. In all of this, Job maintains, there was proof that he was, in fact, leading the life that God had meant him to lead, and he was remaining faithful to the teachings of his religious tradition.

Job's responses, as repetitive as the arguments of the friends in their own way, illustrate another aspect of the artistry of the book. One of the facts of suffering—whether it is physical suffering, pain, nagging discomfort, or debility of a person's physical being, or whether it is mental distress, depression, obsession, betrayal, grief, or unrequited love—is the tendency of the mind to return, again and again, to the fact of pain. To be in pain, in fact, is to be forced to think of pain over and over again. That is one of the painful aspects, so to speak, of pain itself. It is obvious even in relatively minor physical ailments like muscle pain: if the pain is at all severe, it tends to drive out any other thoughts. So much the more is it the case with severe pain, with depression or obsession, and with deep remorse or disappointment. Try as we might, we cannot escape the thought of the torment we are in. Our mind continually returns to the sorrow, the painful thought, or whatever the distress consists of.

This is reflected in the structure of Job's arguments. Over and over again, the same topics are raised and knocked down. In this sense, the book represents not an argument among several human beings, but the mental process that can take place when a person tries to come to terms with a painful situation: "Did I do something wrong?" "Is this my fault?" "Did I deserve this?" "Could I have prevented this?" No matter how many times we review the evidence—and whether the situation was partly our fault or whether we have been stricken "out of the blue" seems to make no difference—the questions arise again and again.

This is part of the "realism" of the text: the reality of Job does not reside in the characters or the situation, both of which are presented in a conventional manner, but in the representation in a literary form of the mental carousel on which most thinking human beings have found themselves at one time or another.

Taking It to Another Level and Moving Past the Arguments

In chapter 24 the book of Job seems to lose its structural organization, and in various ways what happens after that point in the text requires some explanation. We will examine some of those questions here, and treatments of these various issues are also located in the commentary to the translation, such as the rearrangement of material in chapters 24–27. In the book as it stands now, however, there are other matters in chapters 28–41 that do not involve disarray in the text, but rather something else. Three aspects of these chapters involve striking departures from the argument presented in the main section of the book up through the end of chapter 23 and are important to discuss here: the wisdom poem in chapter 28, Elihu's speeches in chapters 32–37, and the speeches of God in chapters 38–41.

The Wisdom Poem

Although chapter 28 is ascribed to Job as the speaker, it can in fact be detached from its context and treated as a separate composition that has simply been inserted by the author (or, less likely, by a later editor). It dramatically shifts the general argument of the book, from an effort to determine whether the world makes any moral sense to an effort to come to grips with the meaning of "wisdom." The chapter's conclusion—that "awe" of God or "reverence" for God ("fear" is not as good a translation) is "wisdom"—is also found in the book of Proverbs (1:7 and elsewhere) and thus sounds very different from what we have heard in Job up until this point.

Chapter 28 is often categorized as a hymn or poem *in praise* of wisdom, but in fact it is a poetic evocation of the *difficulty of obtaining* wisdom. Its argument takes the form of an extended metaphor, speaking first about the dangers of mining for gold, silver, and precious gems. The descriptions of ancient mining techniques and the realistic presentation of the risks and the atmosphere of a mine constitute some of the most stunning poetry in the book. With a spare refrain—"Wisdom—where is it found?"—the poem implicitly compares the enormous efforts and risks that human beings will undertake to find precious gems or metals with our lack of effort in seeking after wisdom. Without saying so directly, the poem argues that wisdom is far more valuable than gold or gems, and so it criticizes the human reluctance to expend even a fraction of our time or energy on attaining wisdom, as compared with our strenuous efforts to seek wealth.

Without any connection to the argument that has gone before—and with no very clear connection to the parts of the book that follow—the wisdom poem nevertheless introduces a perspective that we as its readers are being subtly urged to keep in mind. "What are you willing to do to become wise? Look at the risks people take to find gems or gold—are you willing to take any risk at all to gain the valuable prize of wisdom?"

Such a question does not answer the problem of suffering but looks at it from a different perspective. "What if, through suffering, you can gain insight that you might obtain in no other way? Would it be worth it? Underground the miner braves darkness and danger, even risks death, in the hope of material reward—are you also willing to risk pain and suffering in a quest for deeper insight and knowledge?"

The poem does not answer the question, because it is not a question that can be answered in the abstract. It is an existential question that can only be answered in the context of an individual, lived human life. And, by its very nature, it may be answerable only at the end of life—or not at all. "Was it worth it?" is a very different question from "Will it be worth it?" And in any case, we may never know.

The Elihu Explosion

Chapters 32–37, though they seemingly return to the argument about the justice of suffering, are an interruption in a number of ways. The character who speaks, Elihu, has not been previously introduced. He appears and although (unlike Job) he is given a genealogy, his presence is otherwise unexplained. For the most part Elihu speaks without interruption in these chapters. Unlike Job, who does not address his friends by name, and the friends, who do not address Job by name, Elihu repeats Job's name a number of times, although he mentions no others. When he is finished speaking, he vanishes—no one, including God, mentions him or even alludes to anything he has said.

As odd as the intrusion of Elihu is structurally, it is also something of a misfit thematically. Commenters in the past have criticized the Elihu speeches for their literary quality, judging them to be poetically inferior to the speeches of Job and his friends, of God, and of the wisdom poem in chapter 28. It is not, therefore, simply that these speeches do not seem relevant to the rest of the text, because that objection could also be raised against the poem in praise of wisdom. It is the nature of their *style* that has raised questions. It is repetitive and tends to dwell on one particular point for far too long, well past the time when anything new could be said. So it is difficult to escape the thought that if these Elihu sections are meant as an augmentation of the book, they function partly as a slightly comic interlude before the crashing finale of God's speeches, beginning in chapter 38.

Part of the comical aspect of the Elihu material is the picture of a speaker ranting away while completely unconscious of the way he would appear to the audience. This is true practically from the start of his speeches. Elihu presents himself as one who is about to burst with new words, arguments, and refutations that none of the friends have yet made in their contest with Job. He exhorts Job to hear him, to listen, and at the same time to answer him. He asserts both that God hears the cry of the oppressed and that God doesn't hear it because of human arrogance. He argues that God punishes the wicked, and then he contradicts himself—God does not intervene because human righteousness and human wickedness are of concern only to other human beings, not to God. The anticlimactic nature of his arguments—Elihu says nothing that has not already been said, exhaustively, and manages to take both sides of many of the arguments—is only part of the ludicrous effect. He begins his rant with a conventional apology, claiming he has waited to speak until his elders were finished, out of respect for their age and experience. But he then proceeds to accuse them of losing the argument and letting down God's side. He will show them how to argue God's case effectively. This opening position is the opposite of respectful. And we wait interminably to hear his arguments as he repeats over and over that he will speak, he is about to speak, he's opening his mouth, he'll speak out, and so on. When his arguments do come—that God speaks in different ways, in dreams, in night visions, in afflictions—we hear nothing that we haven't heard before. Amid his protestations that he will refute Job with arguments that Job cannot answer, Elihu offers arguments that Job has already amply refuted.

The only structural significance of the Elihu material, in fact, is that it provides a transition between the arguments about affirming or denying a moral order in the universe to those about the grandeur of creation and the awe-inspiring majesty of God that form the core of the final chapters, the speeches that God makes at the climax of the book. But, in what might be an ironic statement about the quality of Elihu's arguments, he backs into this point, raising it only as it develops out of his previous assertion that God judges and punishes the wicked. "God can do anything," Elihu argues, in effect. "Look! God even creates thunderstorms!" And, in a passage typical of his style, Elihu spends the entirety of chapter 37 elaborating on the image of the thunderstorm, repeating the word "voice" five times. In a final burst of argument, Elihu maintains once more that God is far beyond human understanding, and our only choice is to stand before God in awe, because even the height of human wisdom is as nothing to God. And then Elihu vanishes, never to be mentioned again.

God's Speeches from the Storm

In his speeches Elihu has brought up the thunderstorm as one of the chief natural images of God, and as if to validate that point, the poem presents God as speaking from amid the storm. But unlike Elihu or Job's friends, God does not argue about the rightness or wrongness of a moral order in creation. Instead, God bases the entirety of the argument on the awe-inspiring nature of creation itself, and the complexity and power of its operations.

From the opening question, "Who is this?" (38:2), to the sarcastic catalogue beginning, "Where were you when I formed Earth?" (38:4), to the closing line that Leviathan, such a powerful part of creation that he is subject to God but to nothing else, is "king over all the children of pride" (41:34), God's speeches relentlessly press one point: "You can't possibly have an answer from me because it would be utterly beyond your comprehension." It would almost be fair to summarize these speeches as saying, "It's a God thing—you couldn't understand." The effect of this could be to leave the impression that God is dodging the question. The piling up of instance upon instance of the wonders of creation, however, along with God's questions to Job probing the limits of his experience in the whole reach of creation, and the final introduction of Behemoth and

Leviathan—those marvels of creation who are untamable and incomprehensible, and who express the utter mysteriousness of reality itself—instead serve to move the entire conversation onto another level. The wisdom poem of chapter 28 implies an existential question: "How much are you willing to undergo in order to gain wisdom?" Elihu asks explicitly, "How can you possibly put yourself on the same footing as God?" God's argument takes this point from Elihu and makes it a final terminus for the whole discussion. What is the use of asking whether this whole operation has a point or of asking for the meaning of creation? If there is such a meaning, if there is any point to all of this—if the question even has a meaning that you can grasp—you are simply not among the group that could understand the answer, if in fact there is an answer. Only God can ask the question, not merely because only God can answer it, but also because only God could understand whatever answer there might be.

Problems with the Text

Part of the difficulty of comprehending Job, even after we understand what kind of literary work we are reading, lies in textual problems in the book as a whole that are specific to Job itself. These are primarily of two kinds: problems with the *form* of the book and the way it is organized, and problems seemingly arising from *defects* in the transmission of the actual writing over a long period of time.

Problems with the Form of the Book of Job

PROBLEM 1: HOW DOES THE PROSE FRAME STORY FIT WITH THE POETICAL SECTIONS?

The prose framework tells the story, in the manner of a folktale, of a very righteous man who is the subject, unknown to himself, of what amounts to a bet between God and a heavenly being called "the Satan," the accuser, the opponent. Though greatly provoked—he loses wealth, children, and health—this Job character does not offer any criticism of the suffering to which he has been subjected and defends God's provision of good and evil. In the end, as Job holds steadfast, God rewards him with another family and more possessions than he had lost, including new children to replace the ones who had been killed in the beginning section.

It is clear that the prose frame establishes, once and for all, that Job is not a historical narrative but a *tale* told to make a point. Any suggestion that the story is actually true would involve its readers in trying to defend and explain a God who is morally monstrous, evil, shallow, and obtuse. The offense is not lessened—in fact, it is compounded—by the concluding section, in which the tale essentially presents the gift of new children as compensation for the loss of children in chapter 1. Such an ending verges on the grotesque.

PROBLEM 2: HOW IS THE CHARACTER OF JOB PRESENTED IN DIFFERENT PARTS OF THE BOOK?

Job himself is a different character in the frame and in the dialogue. In the frame, he is pious and submissive, saying very little; in the dialogue, he is irreverent and assertive, with plenty to say. Thus the Job of the dialogue is a much more appealing character than the Job of the prose frame.

The question is whether the prose portions were part of the original composition—written by the author of the dialogue in a "folklore" style in order to set the scene, or perhaps an actual folktale that was simply taken over by the author—or whether it was added by a later and perhaps imperceptive editor to the poetical dialogue. This kind of supplemental editing is not unusual in the different books of the Bible as they were handed down, compiled, and collected through the centuries. It is not possible to come to a final determination about this, but the prose tale does serve some functions: it establishes a situation, provides a moral framework, raises the issues to be discussed, and in general situates the poetical dialogue in an account that helps it make sense.

PROBLEM 3: HOW IS THE CHARACTER OF GOD PRESENTED IN DIFFERENT PARTS OF THE BOOK?

God, too, is a different character in the prose frame and in the poetical dialogue. It is impossible to identify the God of chapters 38–41 with the empty and foolish character of the prose frame. The God who in chapter 1 asks the Satan, in effect, "Don't you think my worshiper Job is terrific?"—like some proud parent with a wallet full of photographs—is simply not the same as the one who thunders, "Where were you when I formed Earth?" (38:4).

PROBLEM 4: WHAT HAPPENS TO THE SATAN CHARACTER?
The Satan is prominent in the first two chapters, setting the whole story in motion, but then disappears, never to be seen or heard from again.

PROBLEM 5: HOW ARE THE PARTS OF THE POETICAL DIALOGUES MEANT TO CONNECT?
Chapter 28, which is Job's speech on the difficulty of finding wisdom, does not seem connected to any of the material before or after it. Elihu's speeches, chapters 32–37, do have a connection to the preceding dialogue, but nothing that follows them seems attached to them. Furthermore, no other character, including God, mentions Elihu or his arguments.

Problems Arising from Defects in Transmission
In addition to these five problems with Job as a poetical composition, there are places where the biblical text itself may be damaged. Some problems that seem to have arisen from its transmission—copying errors, missing text, and so on—are treated in the comments.

PROBLEM 1: WHAT HAPPENED TO THE THIRD POETICAL DIALOGUE?
As the outline of Job indicated, the third dialogue is defective, containing no speech by Zophar and therefore no reply from Job. In addition, Bildad's speech in this cycle is very short (only six verses) and seems to have lost some of its text.

PROBLEM 2: IS JOB INCONSISTENT?
Throughout the dialogues, Job maintains that he has not been treated justly and that, in fact, the world does not show any moral order or any way of rewarding the good and punishing the wicked. Yet in chapter 26, Job seems to change his position: he is praising God, exalting God's

power, and maintaining that our knowledge of God is merely knowledge of the very edges of God's being. In chapter 27, after restating at the beginning his conviction that he has done nothing wrong, Job continues in a very different way, maintaining that the wicked are indeed punished at the hands of God. It may be that this speech, in fact, contains not only Job's words but also those originally written for one of the friends.

Does the Book of Job Have a Theological Point?

Some of the difficulties in the text of Job—omissions, additions and insertions, disorganization, and possible rewritings—seem to be the result of discomfort on the part of the various copyists and editors who had a part in shaping the book into the final form we have before us today. They may have had problems with the arguments, imagery, piety, and language of the poetry itself. Some passages may have been tampered with because these scribes and editors found them blasphemous or insufficiently respectful of God. (Some of these passages are dealt with in the comments.) But in another sense, we can ask the question as well. Is the book of Job really a theological argument that grapples with the problem of suffering and evil in a world created by God? To look at this question is to recognize that we must ask another question first: What would the world look like if it conformed to the religious beliefs of Job's friends, and to the implicit beliefs of Job himself as they are revealed in his protests against what is actually happening to him?

The critique of the world as it stands—and the furious, though futile, defense of moral order that is waged by Job's friends—implies a vision of how the world should work. That vision essentially says that if you worship God (and not any other power or any idol); if you are charitable with whatever wealth you may possess or earn; if you raise your children to be respectful and pious themselves; if you side with the poor and oppressed, feed the hungry, clothe the naked, and house the homeless—if you live in this way, you will be rewarded (or should be) with long life, prosperity, a happy family, and social honors and deference. We can leave aside the objection that if everyone were moral and therefore prosperous, there would be no oppressed or poor people to whom we could be charitable. The point of the vision is not to describe what would happen, but what *ought* to happen. Instead, we can ask ourselves: Well, if the world worked that way, what would it mean?

It would mean, among other things, that a guaranteed way to gain a long life, a happy family, and wealth for yourself and your offspring is to act in certain ways. Acting charitably and relieving distress would, in essence, be a sure way to gain prosperity. For at least some of us, therefore, helping the hungry and homeless wouldn't be something we do because it is ethical and right, but because it would make us rich, happy, and long-lived. The danger of a universe like that, set up to reward virtuous behavior with positive consequences, is to make virtuous behavior a matter of self-interest rather than of character. In other words, we would act virtuously not because virtue is good in itself and we should practice it no matter what the consequences, but because virtue would result in a good external to itself.

Ultimately, then, the critique of the book of Job, though it starts out by saying that life is unfair, turns into a much deeper critique—one that asks *why* we want life to be fair. Do we value fairness for its own sake? Or do we want fairness to result in something else that we value more, which is wealth, happiness, and a long life?

The theological point of the book of Job, therefore, if it can be said to have a theology, is to make us aware of the impossibility of creating a moral universe that at one and the same time would bring us to desire goodness for its own sake *and* reward us extrinsically for being good. This is the book of Job's unique moral insight. Acting justly and generously can, of course, end up benefiting the person who acts as well as those who benefit from such behavior. But it cannot invariably do so without the unintended consequence that we will act in virtuous ways for the sake of rewards that have nothing to do with virtue. Even God cannot square that circle.

The End of It

The final chapter of Job seems to undercut everything that has gone before. After all those chapters of argument, cursing, refutation, and blame—"Life is fair!" versus "Life is not fair!"—God ends up rewarding Job with twice the possessions and all of the family that he had before.

Has the book, therefore, fumbled its very point, the very reason it seems to have been written? Has it made the point that we must not expect virtue to lead inevitably to prosperity, only to turn around and provide an ending to the story that implies exactly the opposite?

It would seem that the book of Job has knocked down its own main point in just this way. But that is not all there is to it. Job is not being rewarded for his good deeds before calamity struck, but for something else. That something else is his refusal to blind himself to reality, and to lie about what he knew to be true, simply to protect what he thought of as God's good reputation. This is what Job's comforters have done, and it lies behind God's denunciation of them as having spoken untruthfully about God's self. In a final ironic twist, the friends themselves are judged harshly and are only rescued by the prayer of a virtuous man: "My servant Job will pray for you; I will countenance his prayer and not treat you according to your folly; because you have not spoken rightly about me, as my servant Job has" (42:8). This is exactly the situation described by Eliphaz in his final speech in chapter 22. So the final lesson with which God leaves the friends, and us, is the exhortation "Don't tell lies about me! Even if you think my reputation is at stake, speak the truth!"

God rebukes Job in the speeches in chapters 38–41. But the essence of the rebuke is that Job has asked for answers that he cannot possibly understand. Nevertheless, given the light that he has, Job has remained faithful to that light and has not attempted to blind himself to the limited truth that he is able to see. Therefore Job is better off than his friends, and Job's seeming blasphemy is more pleasing to God than the friends' conventional piety.

For readers who do not believe in God, the moral is that true religious belief does not, and cannot, mean believing what is not only false but what also goes against the very evidence that is in front of our faces. For readers who do believe in God, the warning is even more severe. We cannot—we must not—ever think that we are the guardians of God's reputation. We must speak the truth, even if it seems damaging to our beliefs. If God's ultimate values include truth, then we cannot base our faith in God on something that is false. Learning the truth can only ultimately bring us closer to God, no matter how far away from us God may seem in that moment when we learn a new truth. God will have the truth, and God will not accept anything less than whatever truth we can perceive, and we cannot run counter to that reality.

Except for brief responses to God, this is the end: "Job's words cease."

A Note on the Translation

The text of the book of Job is very difficult, partly because it is imperfect in various places and partly because it contains many unusual words—in some cases, words that do not appear anywhere else in the Hebrew text of the Bible. I am not a scholar of ancient Near Eastern languages, and the translation is not meant to be a contribution to the scholarly conversation about the difficulties of the text of Job. It is, instead, intended to be as clear as possible for general readers who want to read the book as a poetic and philosophical meditation on various themes. Occasionally, my commentary will offer paraphrases of the text, when it was not clear what the text was trying to get across and no translation seemed to work. I have relied on many other sources for this translation, and they are given in the bibliographical listing at the end of the book. But discussion of the textual difficulties and the citation of words from other ancient Near Eastern languages that might help in the interpretation of the text are out of place in a work intended for a general audience.

There are, however, a few matters having to do with translation choices that I can make clear. I have kept to the standard in English Bibles of using the spelling "LORD" with a capital "L" and small capitals for the other letters when the Hebrew text uses the divine name, *YHVH*. When the Hebrew text is read aloud, this name is not pronounced, but the word *Adonai*, meaning "my Lord," is substituted. The English translation convention is a way of expressing this same care for religious sensibility.

In most of the book, God is referred to by using some terms that essentially all mean "God" or "Divine Being"—*El*, *Eloah*, and so on—or one other Hebrew word, *Shaddai*. This latter word may refer to strength or power, which is how it has been traditionally understood. It is therefore often translated "the Almighty." I find it unfortunate that the word as thus used seems to imply omnipotence, because I do not think *Shaddai* means that. I have therefore chosen to translate it "the Mighty One," capitalized to show that it refers to God.

"The Satan," the character who in the first two chapters sets the plot of the book going, I have rendered as "the Provoker." In the book of Job, the Hebrew word *Satan* is not a proper name but a title, "the Adversary" or "the Accuser." The Satan seems to be the heavenly being who, on behalf of God, tests or tries human beings to assess their true worth. Because it is this character who initiates the plot and who attempts to prod Job into abandoning his piety and devotion to God, I have thought that "Provoker" gets that point across most clearly.

The Hebrew word *Sheol*, the realm of the dead, I have generally rendered as "the Pit." That seems to me to convey what the Hebrew is getting across with the word *Sheol*: the place where dead people go, the dump of the afterlife. It is not a reverent term, but *Sheol* is not a reverent concept. It is not hell, but it certainly isn't heaven. It's almost nothing.

I hope readers will find the translation open and welcoming, but Job is a difficult book and the translation is unavoidably difficult in places.

I have tried to render things as if they were being said by actual human beings—thus I have used contractions where it seemed fitting. I have not, however, tried to make the lines of poetry equal in length or containing a set number of stresses, or anything of that sort. Hebrew poetry is extremely terse, and there is no way to reproduce that in English. The point of the translation is to be as understandable as possible.

The Prose Framework: Opening

Chapters 1 and 2 of the book of Job open with a story that establishes the situation and provides a context for the poetic dialogues that will follow. Many readers object strenuously to this narrative, which portrays God as foolish and boastful, an egocentric who is perfectly willing to destroy the life of a faithful adherent in order to prove a point. The story, for such readers, is also a gross miscarriage of justice not merely for Job, whose family, livelihood, possessions, and ultimately health are ruined, but also for the family members, servants, and animals whose deaths form the basis of Job's sufferings. Such readers usually put their objection in the form of a question: "How could God have done this?"

The usual answer to this question is the observation that this prose framework, serving as the opening of the book of Job, is simply a story, a fictional narrative meant to set the scene for the argument that follows. We are not meant to "take it seriously" any more than we are meant to take literally the narrative that has the prophet Jonah living for three days inside the belly of a great fish. Like the book of Jonah, Job is only a "What if?" tale. What if there were a truly just man who suffered greatly? What would such a man say about his situation, and how would he react to it? Would there be any reason why he might deserve his suffering?

Within the story itself, this is the proper response. But in a larger context, it leaves out a very important qualification. The question for readers like us is not "How could God have done this?" but rather "How *can* God do this?"

✍ Innocent people suffer everywhere, every day. All around us, all over the world, there are people who, though they may not be blameless, have not committed any great evil. Yet they mourn beloved family members, see their property and lives destroyed in natural calamities or the chaos of war, and lose their health and their livelihoods. In short, they are, for no reason, suffering all the calamities that Job suffers. This existential aspect of the book is one of the reasons that people have returned to it with undiminished interest in every generation and have struggled with the questions that it raises for twenty-five centuries.

1 The opening, *ish hayah*, literally "a man there was," differs from the more frequent narrative form *vayyehi ish*, "it came about [that] a man," or in the traditional rendering, "and it came to pass, a man...." Thus the initial words of Job begin a new story rather than continuing a story in progress.

2 A vague reference either to the north (Aram) or the east (Edom). Job does not live in Israel, though he worships the LORD.

3 *Iyov*: Forms of the name Job are found in writings from before 1000 BCE. It may have been chosen for the hero of this work in order to place him not only in a geographically vague place but also one distant in time: "long ago and far away."

4 The paired terms—"blameless" or "perfect, without blemish," and "upright" or "straight"—are meant as mutual modifiers. Not only is Job without a fault in a passive sense, but he is also righteous in action. He is flawless, as an animal meant for sacrifice should be; he is also moral in all his dealings.

5 The usual translation, "fear," does not convey the religious overtones (reverence, respect); in Leviticus 19:3, the same verb is used in an exhortation to "reverence" one's parents—not to fear them, but to treat them with the respect they deserve.

☐ Chapter 1

1 Once there was a man[1] in Uz-land[2] named Job.[3] This man was downright upright,[4] in awe[5] of God, and turning from evil.

(continued on page 5)

3

6 All Job's household inhabitants are numbered in tens or multiples of ten, expressing completeness. In the case of his children, they total ten. Then we have seven thousand plus three thousand, and five hundred plus five hundred.

7 The anniversary of his birthday.

8 Job's sacrifices and prayers on behalf of his children, even for inadvertent or hidden faults, may seem to us overscrupulous. It is certainly meant to convey Job's extreme piety.

9 Literally, "all the days."

10 Literally, "sons of God," meaning not divine offspring but members of the divine council, similar to the council or advisors of an earthly king.

11 When printed in this fashion, following a long-established practice in English-language Bibles, this use of LORD means that the underlying Hebrew text uses four Hebrew letters, *YHVH*, known as the Tetragrammaton, to signify (but not speak) the divine name.

12 The Hebrew word *satan* means "opponent," "accuser," or "adversary." It is not a proper name, and we should not read it in the light of its later development, including that reflected in the Christian Scriptures, of Satan as a demonic spiritual being opposed to God and to the good angels fighting on God's behalf. Instead, the Provoker's task is to test or try people in order to reveal their true selves.

13 God's words echo the description of Job from verse 1, "downright upright, in awe of God, and turning from evil."

14 Literally, "house" or "household."

15 Literally, the text reads "bless," though it is meant to be read as "curse"; this is a way of avoiding actually writing the phrase "curse God."

16 The plot is initiated. In this first stage, the Provoker can cause Job to lose everything around him but must spare him any physical injury.

2 To him were born seven sons and three daughters. 3 He owned seven thousand sheep, three thousand camels, five hundred yoke of oxen, five hundred donkeys, and numerous servants. This man was greater than all other people in the east.**6**

4 His sons, each in turn, gave feasts, each at his home on his day;**7** and they called on their sisters to eat and to drink wine with them.

5 As the days of each feast went by, Job took care to sanctify his children:**8** he would arise of a morning, offer sacrifices for each of them—"because," Job said, "maybe my children sinned and cursed God in their hearts"—all of which Job always**9** did.

6 Now one day, the heavenly beings**10** assembled themselves before the LORD,**11** the Provoker**12** among the rest. 7 The LORD said to the Provoker, "Where have you been?" The Provoker answered the LORD, and said:

"Roaming about the world,
back and forth in it."

8 The LORD said to the Provoker:

"Have you laid to heart
my servant Job? He has no
equal in the world,
downright upright,
holding me in awe,
turning from evil."**13**

9 The Provoker answered the LORD, and said, "Does Job hold God in awe for nothing? 10 Haven't you fenced him round? Him and his family, servants, possessions?**14** Haven't you favored what he does until his flocks cover the earth? 11 But now—reach out and hit it all and he is bound to curse**15** you to your face." 12 So the LORD said to the Provoker, "Lo, the whole of it is in your hands—but do not touch him." And the Provoker left the LORD.**16**

(continued on page 7)

17 Here probably meaning bedouins or nomads. Such raids were always a possibility, especially for outlying settlements.

18 Farmhands or servants; literally, "boys, lads."

19 Repetition for emphasis—one person only escapes from each disaster. Melville alludes to this phrasing in the closing pages of *Moby Dick*.

20 Lightning. The disasters alternate between ones caused by human evil (thieving raids, war) and ones resulting from natural disasters (lightning, windstorms).

21 Job is not saying he will actually return to the womb, as the traditional rendering ("naked will I return") implies. By "there" he means "death" or "the grave."

13 Now one day his sons and daughters were feasting and drinking wine at their oldest brother's house. 14 A messenger came to Job and said, "The oxen were plowing and donkeys grazing near at hand, 15 and Sabeans[17] attacked and carried them away. The fellows[18] they put to the sword and killed. I, I alone,[19] escaped to tell you."

16 He still spoke and another came and said, "God's fire[20] fell from the heavens, burned up the sheep and the fellows completely. I, I alone, escaped to tell you."

17 He still spoke and another came and said, "Chaldeans in three bandit-gangs swept down and carried away the camels, and the fellows they put to the sword and killed. I, I alone, escaped to tell you."

18 He still spoke and another came and said, "Your sons and daughters were eating and drinking wine at the oldest brother's house. 19 Lo, a great wind came from across the desert and struck the four corners of the house. It collapsed on the youths and they are dead. I, I alone, escaped to tell you."

20 Job stood, tore his robe, shaved his head, fell to the ground, and worshiped. 21 He said, "Naked I came from my mother's womb; naked I will depart and go there.[21] The LORD gave, the LORD took—blessed be the LORD's name."

22 In all this Job did not sin, for he did not accuse God of wrong.

1 The Hebrew literally says "Skin for skin," a proverbial phrase meaning something like "He'd give up everything else to save his own skin." The Provoker is making the point that Job still honors God because God has not touched Job's own person—just those of his family, his household, and all his possessions.

☐ Chapter 2

1 The day came when the heavenly beings assembled themselves before the LORD. The Provoker presented himself among them. 2 The LORD said to the Provoker, "Where have you been?" The Provoker answered the LORD and said:

> "Roaming about the world,
> back and forth in it."

3 The LORD said to the Provoker:

> "Have you laid to heart
> my servant Job?
> He has no equal in the world,
> downright upright,
> holding me in awe,
> turning from evil.
> He still holds his wholeness,
> though you prodded me against him,
> to ruin him for no reason."

4 The Provoker answered the LORD:

> "All, save his skin, to save his skin!¹
> A man gives all that he has for his life.
> 5 Reach out and hit him!
> To the bone, to the flesh!
> He's bound to curse you to your face."

(continued on page 11)

9

2 Literally, "bless." See chapter 1, note 15.

3 This has been taken in two ways. It is read as meaning either "Job didn't *say* anything against God, though he might have had impious thoughts" or (as is probably the case) "Job guarded himself so as not to let a word against God rest for a moment even on his lips." It could therefore be translated either as "sin visibly" or as "sin by so much as a murmur."

4 Eliphaz the Temanite is from the south (Teman is "southland"), and his name may mean "God is gold." Bildad the Shuhite may be from southern Arabia; it is not clear what his name means. Zophar the Naamathite is also likely meant to be from Arabia; his name might mean "young bird," and he is the least vocal of the friends, always speaking last (and, in the Hebrew text, having no speech at all during the third cycle).

5 A sign of abasement before Job's grief; the dust or dirt from the ground, placed on the highest part of the brow, symbolizes lowering the head to the point below the level of the feet.

6 The LORD said to the Provoker:
"He's in your hands.
But spare his life."

7 The Provoker left the LORD's presence and struck Job with painful sores from the soles of his feet to his head. 8 He took a piece of crockery to scrape himself, sitting in the ashes.
9 His wife said to him:
"Still holding your wholeness?
Curse² God and die!"

10 And he said to her:
"You talk like fool women talk.
Do we take good from God,
but not take trouble?"

In all of this Job did not sin with his lips.³
11 When Job's three friends heard about all of the trouble that came upon him, each set out from his home: Eliphaz of Teman, Bildad of Shuha, Zophar of Naamath.⁴ They met one another and went to him to offer sympathy and comfort. 12 Even seeing him from far off, they could hardly recognize him. They wept loudly. Each tore his robe. They sprinkled dust on the tops of their heads.⁵ 13 They sat on the ground with him seven days and seven nights. Not one said a word to him; they saw his trouble was very great.

Job's Curse

In direct contradiction to the picture of Job presented in chapters 1 and 2, Job lifts up his voice and curses in a poetical and scathing outcry of bitterness for the fact of his life. Job's language is relentless and in places painfully rude. He curses not only the very day of his birth, but also the night of the sexual act that brought about his conception, his emergence from the womb, his nurture, and the fact that he has not died.

1 The time of Job's conception. Not content merely to curse the day of his birth, he goes back and curses the darkness of the sexual intercourse of his parents.

2 Literally, "barren," as in Isaiah 49:21.

3 The Hebrew *renanah* means "joyful, exultant shout," as in Psalm 100:2, "Worship the LORD with gladness; come into God's presence with a shout of joy [or 'with singing']." The same word occurs in Job 20:5, "the glee of the wicked." Here it is meant to indicate the cry of sexual release; Job wishes the act of intercourse, and hence this cry, had never occurred.

4 An obscure reference to ancient Near Eastern mythologies of the battle between the chief god of the pantheon and the chaotic sea. In effect Job is asking those who cursed the Sea and the monster of the sea, Leviathan—the curse that was, he thinks, instrumental in their defeat—to curse just as effectively the day of his birth. "Sea" (Hebrew, *yam*) is a conjecture for the text's reading *yom* (day), which does not make sense.

5 Literally, "doors of my womb," that is, "the opening of my mother's womb."

☐ Chapter 3

1 Then Job opened his mouth and damned his day. 2 He said:
3 "Cursed the day I was born!
the night[1] that said, 'A male made!'
4 Dark be that day—
God on high find it meaningless—
on it shed no light—
5 dark deep gloom seize it,
cloud darken it,
day's blackness frighten it!

6 "That night—murk grab it,
do not count it in days of the year,
do not enter it in any month.
7 Look! May that night be empty,[2]
bearing no cry of climax.[3]
8 May those cursing Sea curse it,[4]
those who waken Leviathan.
9 May its morning stars darken;
may it wait vainly for light,
never see the eyelids of morn.

10 "For it did not close the womb-lips,[5]
it hid no trouble from my eyes.
11 Why did I not die at birth,
perish as I dropped from the womb?

(continued on page 17)

6   The mother's or midwife's lap, which catches the infant as it emerges from the birth canal. It may also mean the acceptance of the child by the father, when the father places the child on his knees.

7   This rather obscure passage (verses 13–15) seems to mean that had Job never lived, he would be as peaceful as the most successful ruler or potentate, who had lived a life full of accomplishment and then died in peace.

8   The voice of the slave-master.

12 Why did knees catch me,[6]
breasts suckle me?
13 Else now I would lie quietly,
sleeping and resting,
14 as do kings and the world's counsel
who build upon ruins,
15 or rulers with gold
who fill houses with silver.[7]

16 "Would I were hid like the stillborn,
or infants who never saw light.
17 There the wicked trouble no more;
those whose strength is spent can rest.
18 Captives are at ease,
no longer hear the driver's voice.[8]
19 Lowly and great are there,
and slave is free from master.

20 "Why does God give light to the miserable,
life to bitter souls—
21 who vainly long for death,
search for it more than buried treasure,
22 are glad and joyful,
happy to reach the grave—
23 life to one whose path is hidden,
whom God constrains?
24 I have sighs for food,
groans for drink,
25 fearsome fear befell me,
what I dreaded came upon me.
26 I have no peace, I have no quiet,
I have no rest—turmoil came."

The First Dialogue Cycle

Eliphaz's first speech occurs in chapters 4–5 and is the longest of the friends' speeches (all of the others are no longer than one chapter); it is fairly complex. After an opening exhortation to Job to heed the advice he has, in the past, given to others (4:3–6), Eliphaz turns to his main argument. It has three parts: the assertion that God's care for the innocent and judgment on the guilty is certain (4:7–11); his account of a personal revelation of the divine righteousness amid the troubles of human life (4:12–5:7); and a return to his opening claim that God will ultimately intervene in human life for good and against evil (5:8–27).

1 The word means "over-hasty" and conveys a reaction to sudden disaster.

2 "Of God" is not in the text but is understood.

3 "Those who go straight."

4 Evil or trouble.

5 Though a roaring lion seeking prey may seem to be extremely powerful, in fact its offspring are vulnerable, and the lion itself may fail to catch and kill its prey, thereby starving its cubs. In the same way, a wicked person might seem impregnable to us but in fact may be destroyed by misfortune.

□ Chapter 4

1 Eliphaz the Temanite answered:
  2 "Will you weary of words if one dares to speak?
  Who can hold back?

  3 "Lo, you tutored many;
  strengthened feeble hands;
  4 encouraged the tottering;
  bolstered the weak-kneed.
  5 But now! It's on you and you sink!
  It hits home and you're shocked![1]
  6 Isn't awe of God[2] your reliance?
  Aren't upright ways your hope?

  7 "Think about this! What innocent one perished?
  Where were moral ones[3] destroyed?
  8 I have indeed seen those planning evil,
  sowing trouble, reap it;[4]
  9 with one divine breath they perish;
  in one angry gust they wither.
  10 A lion roars—the great cat calls—
  yet the young lions' teeth are broken.
  11 The lion perishes, lacking prey;
  the lioness's cubs are scattered.[5]

(continued on page 23)

6 Verses 12–21 are Eliphaz's description of a mysterious and terrifying nighttime revelation. This is one of the most evocative passages in the Bible for its depiction of the numinous, that eerie and compelling feeling that we are in the presence of a spiritual or otherworldly dimension.

7 This word signals that the speaker is moving to another subject. Eliphaz has briefly laid out his belief that God's justice ultimately triumphs in this world, rewarding the virtuous and punishing or foiling the wicked. He turns here to another source of knowledge, over and above that of his observation and experience of human life: a revelation from beyond.

8 The passive form implies a divine action, a way of evoking God without naming God.

9 The Hebrew word *ruach* can mean "spirit," "wind," or "breath."

10 This verse can be read either as two rhetorical questions—Are human beings more righteous than God? Are they more pure than the One who made them?—or as a direct quotation of the divine voice. If the latter is correct, it is not clear whether the speaker is God or an angelic or heavenly being.

11 Because God does not trust even the heavenly beings, how much less will God trust human beings? This quick series of images effectively evokes the fragility and brevity of human life.

12 Die without ever having gained wisdom.

12⁶ "Now!⁷—a word was brought⁸ to me in secret;
its whisper caught my ear—
13 in anxious dreams of night,
when sleep of depth falls upon us—
14 Terror held me!—trembling—
it shook all my bones!
15 A breath⁹ slid past my face;
the hairs of my skin prickled.
16 A shape—I couldn't make it out—
paused before my eyes;
grew still; then, I heard a voice:
17 'Is mortal righteousness more than divine?
Is human purity more than the Maker's?'¹⁰
18 Lo, God doesn't trust even God's own servants—
calls God's messengers on their faults—
19 much less those in clay houses,¹¹
built on dust,
pulverized like a moth,
20 broken before dawn becomes dusk,
not even so much as known before they perish,
21 tent cords uprooted,
they die without wisdom."¹²

1 Eliphaz now returns to addressing Job directly.

2 "Holy ones" refers to lesser heavenly beings who might intercede on Job's behalf.

3 Anger that flares up suddenly, "jealousy," or "envy," from a word that means "redden with emotion." The images convey what happens when we do not control our emotions, but are rather blown this way and that by them.

4 The Hebrew reads "I cursed"; the translation is based on a conjecture.

5 His children have no recourse against unjust rulings. Disputes over civil law were argued in front of elders sitting in "the gate," which was the area near the entry to the city where its leading citizens gathered to adjudicate.

6 This passage is obscure. It seems to mean that the hungry ("desperate") and the thirsty ("grasping") will utterly consume the wealth of any man who gains a fortune he does not deserve.

7 The traditional rendering of this verse is "Man is born for trouble as the sparks fly upward." The "sparks" or "flames" are literally "sons of *resheph*," a god of pestilence.

8 Keeping them from succeeding to achieve their own good or in carrying out plans aimed at the misfortune of others.

☐ Chapter 5

1 "Call away![1] Who will answer?
To which of the holy ones[2] will you turn?
2 Hasty temper kills the fool,
jealousy[3] slays the simple.
3 Indeed I have seen[4] the fool take root,
but his dwelling was damned,
4 his offspring unsaved,
crushed in the gate with no defense.[5]
5 The desperate devour his harvest,
right down to the thorns,
and the grasping gulp down his wealth.[6]
6 Does not sorrow spring up from soil,
trouble sprout from the ground?

7 "Human beings indeed are born for trouble,
sparks of sickness flying up.[7]
8 But were I thus, I'd seek for God,
before God lay my case—
9 who does great things, unsearchable,
wondrous things uncountable,
10 giving rain to earth's face,
waters to the field's face,
11 raising the lowly ones,
lifting mourners to safety.
12 God foils crafty plans,
keeping their hands from success,[8]

(continued on page 27)

9 The Hebrew reads "from their mouth."

10 The Hebrew word is *Shaddai*, a divine title, usually translated as "Almighty." The suggestion of omnipotence, however, is not present in the Hebrew word.

11 The Hebrew is taken to be *sed* (demon) rather than *sod* (destruction).

12 The Hebrew reads *eben*, "stones," but substituting *adon*, "spirits," in the sense of "sources of fertility," fits the overall sense better.

13 catches even the wise in their own craft,
sweeping the conniving schemes away.
14 In daylight darkness shadows them,
they feel their way at noon as at midnight.
15 God saves the simple[9] from the sword,
the needy from the grasp of the strong,
16 so there is hope for the poor,
and evil's mouth shuts.

17 "Lo, the mortal is fortunate in divine correction,
so do not downplay the discipline of the Mighty One.[10]
18 God indeed wounds, but God bandages,
God injures, but God's hands heal.
19 Through six disasters God will bring you safely,
through seven no evil come upon you.
20 In famine God will rescue you from death,
And in warfare from sword-stroke.
21 You will be guarded from incantation,
you will not fear the demon's[11] advent.
22 You will laugh at ruin and famine,
you will not fear any earthly beast.
23 You will covenant with the field-spirits,[12]
wild animals will be at peace with you.
24 You will know your tent is safe,
you will look over your property and not be short.
25 You will know your many children,
descendants like field-grass.
26 You will come in full strength right to the grave,
like the harvested sheaf in season.
27 Lo, we have tested and tried this: It is thus!
Hear it and take it to heart!"

⟨ꝏ⟩ Chapters 6–7 present Job's reply. In the first part of this lengthy response to Eliphaz's speech, Job reacts first to his actual experience of misery and loss (6:1–7) and then specifically to the words of Eliphaz (6:8–30). Job then embarks on a description of human existence as slavery (7:1–7) and of God as a slave-master (7:8–21). In the second part of chapter 7 particularly, Job's challenge to God becomes daring and provocative.

1 In verses 2–3, Job mockingly echoes Eliphaz ("Hasty temper kills the fool," 5:2). The rhetorical arrangement of these verses can be confusing. A paraphrase indicates how they are to be read: "If you put my hasty temper on one side of the scales, and my misery on the other side, my misery would outweigh all the sands of the seas; therefore, my misery also outweighs my hasty words and makes them excusable."

2 Hebrew, *Shaddai*.

3 When animals are given their proper food, they do not "bray" or "bellow." So the fact that Job is complaining is therefore evidence that he has not been given "food" (that is, words from Eliphaz) that is fitting or proper for him, but instead has been fed "tasteless slime" (verse 6).

4 The image is of something both insipid and nauseating, like raw egg white, that makes the gorge rise—such is Job's reaction to being subjected to the speech of Eliphaz.

5 "Throat" in Hebrew is *nephesh*, often translated "soul"; it represents the neck and upper chest, where breath resides.

6 "Your words" is supplied in the translation; the Hebrew reads simply "they."

7 A plea for death (see Job's curse on his own existence in chapter 3).

☐ Chapter 6

1 Job answered:
    2 "Were my hasty temper weighed,
    my misery piled on the scales,
    3 surely it outweighs the sea-sands,
    and thus my words rush out.[1]
    4 For the Mighty One's[2] arrows are in me;
    my spirit gulps their venom,
    God's terrors are arrayed against me.

    5 "Does the wild ass bray over grass?
    Does the ox bellow over feed?[3]
    6 Do we eat bland food without salt?
    Is there flavor in tasteless slime?[4]
    7 My throat[5] revolts at its touch;
    your words[6] are sickening food.
    8 O, may my plea[7] be answered—
    may God give what I hope for:
    9 that God be willing to crush me,
    that God free God's hand and cut my thread!

(continued on page 31)

8 Job refers to the pain of childbirth, here used ironically of being "born" into death.

9 A paraphrase to bring out the sense; literally, "that I never denied the words of the Holy One."

10 Meaning "Am I impervious to God's blows?"

11 Echoing 5:12, "keeping their hands from success."

12 Literally, "brothers."

13 The argument here is that these "friends" are like "gulches" (the Hebrew *nachal* means a seasonal watercourse, a wadi) that flood during the spring rains and snowmelt but then dry up in the summer heat of Job's need.

14 By association of ideas, Job argues that as the gulch dries out when the spring rains and thaw are over, so do caravans passing through the desert dry out because they are misled by mirages and fail to find the water they are seeking.

10 That would console me—
I would joy in the writing pain—**8**
the Holy One owes me as much, since I never denied God.**9**

11 "Where is my power to endure this?
To what end should I prolong my life?
12 Am I strong as stone?
Is my flesh hard as bronze?**10**
13 Do I have any inner reserves?
Lasting success has fled from me.**11**

14 "Friends**12** should be loyal to a failing one—
even if he abandons awe of the Mighty One.
15 But my friends are unreliable, gulches
now empty, now overflowing—
16 dense with ice-melt,
swollen with snow,
17 then going dry in a season,
evaporating in the heat.**13**
18 Caravans forsake their way,
turn into the desert—to their death!
19 Caravans of Tema seek,
travelers of Sheba hope,
20 but, their trust traduced,
they arrive at disappointment.**14**

(continued on page 33)

15   The friends are like empty watercourses or mirages in the desert.

16   An orphan who is treated as a slave and sold off to pay a dead parent's debt.

17   Job's argument is that he can tell when he is being subjected to nonsense.

21 "Such were you—nothing![15]
Seeing dread, you fear!
22 Have I asked you, 'Give to me!'
'Pay my ransom with your goods!'
23 'Save me from my enemy!'
'Redeem me from ruthless captives!'?

24 "Teach me—I'll keep quiet.
Show me where I went wrong.
25 How pleasant are your honest thoughts!
But what does your argument prove?
26 You speak to correct me,
call my despairing speech wind.
27 You'd flip a coin to win an orphan,[16]
haggle over a friend.

28 "Please! Look at me!
Would I lie to your faces?
29 Now turn! Stop finding me guilty!
Turn! See my righteousness!
30 Is there guilt on my lips?
Can't my mouth taste your false words?"[17]

1 Hebrew, *Sheol*, the place of departed spirits, where existence is shadowy, verging on nonexistence (similar to the Greek idea of Hades).

☐ Chapter 7

1 "Does not everyone have hard labor on earth?
Are not their days like those of day-laborers?
2 A slave who pants for shade—
a day-laborer eager to be paid—
3 so empty months come to me,
wearisome nights are paid to me.
4 When I lie down I wonder,
'How long until I rise?'
The night stretches
and I stretch and turn until dawn.
5 My flesh is covered with maggots and scabs,
my skin is split and festering.
6 My days flit faster than the weaver's shuttle;
they pass by hopelessly.

7 "Remember! My life is but breath;
my eye will not again see good.
8 No seeing eye will spot me;
your eye is on me, and I'm gone.
9 A cloud slips off, is gone;
one who goes down to the Pit[1] does not return.
10 He comes back no more to his house,
his place knows him no more.

(continued on page 37)

2 The forces of chaos that God had to subdue at creation. Since Job is in no way a similar threat or challenge to God's reign, he does not deserve the same amount of divine attention and power.

3 The bed provides as much "comfort" to Job in his distress as does the friends' "consolation," despite their offer in 2:11. Job is again sarcastic.

4 God.

5 Perhaps a representation of the words of one "strangling" (verse 15).

6 Hebrew *hevel*, "puff," "mere breath"—what is evanescent, ungraspable, momentary. In the book of Ecclesiastes, the traditional translation for this word is "vanity," emptiness. See also Psalm 39:5, 39:11 (Hebrew verses 6 and 12).

7 See Psalm 39:13: "Turn your gaze away from me, that I may smile again."

8 A request for a brief respite, similar to "Give me a minute!"

9 Apparently an interpolation; it does not seem to fit the line.

10 The Hebrew reads "a burden to myself," which is probably a change put in by a religious copyist ("to me" being substituted for "to you," so as not to make any accusation against God or imply that God is affected by Job's suffering). The original wording, followed here, is in the ancient Greek version, the Septuagint.

11 "Thus I will not silence my mouth.
I will speak in agony of spirit,
complain in the bitterness of life.
12 Am I the sea? Am I the Deep Monster
that you set watch over me?**2**
13 When I say, 'My bed will console me,
my couch ease my complaint,'**3**
14 you**4** then frighten me with dreams,
scare me with nightmares—
15 thus my breath chooses strangling,
death rather than a body.
16 I loathe—I would not live forever—**5**
Let me alone! My days are empty.**6**

17 "What are human beings, that you made them great,
that in your heart you attend to them,
18 that morning by morning you inspect them,
moment by moment test them?
19 Can't you look away from me?**7**
Let me alone to swallow my spit?**8**

20 *"[How have I sinned?]***9**
What have I done to you? Watcher!
Why have you made me your target?
How did I become your burden?**10**
21 Why can't you pardon my offenses?
Forgive my sin?
I'll soon be asleep in the dust.
You'll look for me, but I will be no more."

In Bildad's first speech, he first questions what Job has maintained all along—"So! God twists justice?"—and then invokes ancestral wisdom. Job's children may well have deserved their punishment, but in any event neither Job nor any other individual human being can live long enough to gain the understanding necessary for answering Job's complaint. Instead, we must rely on the accumulated wisdom of past generations. Bildad makes his argument—that ultimately those who are virtuous will come out on top—by means of a comparison, a parable of two plants. One plant may seem to flourish, like the wicked, but ultimately will wither, with no more strength than a spider's web or a shaky house (verses 11–15). The other, with water and sunlight, flourishes, and even if adversity comes (verse 18), it will regrow to be as healthy as it was before.

1 Or "perverts."

☐ Chapter 8

1 Bildad the Shuhite answered:
    2 "How long will you speak thus?
    The speech of your mouth is just wind.

    3 "So! God twists[1] justice?
    The Mighty One twists righteousness?
    4 If your children sinned against God,
    God handed them over to their guilt.
    5 If you will look to God
    and beg the Mighty One,
    6 if you are pure and upright,
    even now God will stir God's self for you,
    and restore you to your right place.

    7 "Thus where you began will be humble
    compared to how greatly your future will prosper.
    8 Ask the former generation,
    discover what the fathers learned:
    9 We are here but a day, knowing nothing;
    our days on earth are a shadow.
    10 Won't they instruct you? Won't they tell you?
    Won't they bring out words from their understanding?
    11 Will the papyrus grow without a marsh?
    Will reeds spread without water?
    12 Growing, still uncut,
    they'd wither like grass.

(continued on page 41)

2 Referring to one who relies on wickedness, which is ultimately no stronger than a spider's web.

3 The metaphor (verses 16–19) is of a twining plant—perhaps an invasive vine—overgrowing a plot of land, even the stones, during the rainy season. But it sinks from sight in the dry season, so that the land no longer remembers it, and something else grows there instead.

4 This is meant ironically.

13 "Thus the destiny of all who forget God;
so profane hopes die.
14 He[2] trusts in a thread,
relies on a spider's web.
15 He leans on his house, but it doesn't stand;
he clings, but it doesn't hold.
16 He is a well-watered plant[3] in sunshine,
spreading new growth over the garden,
17 twining roots around the rocks,
looking for a house in the stones.

18 "But when he sinks from the place
it disowns him: 'I never saw you.'
19 Lo, the joy[4] of his way:
others grow from the soil.
20 Lo, God does not reject the upright
nor strengthen the power of evildoers.
21 God will fill your mouth with laughter,
your lips with joyous cries.
22 Those who hate you will be covered in shame,
the tent of the wicked be no more."

In Job's response, he accepts Eliphaz's assertion (4:17) that before God, no human being can be righteous. But he turns this around, and makes it the key to his argument: "Yes, I agree, not one of us is equal to God—in righteousness or in anything else. How could we be? God far exceeds us in wisdom, in power, in creativity. Even if we were righteous, God could crush us; even if we could argue with God, we would lose. There is no independent place where we could meet; no arbiter who stands above both sides and could judge impartially." So Job then makes the key point of his argument: "God, if you are condemning me—if all this suffering is making the point that I've fallen short in some way—then please tell me what I have done! Otherwise, what was the point of bringing me into existence at all?" Chapter 9 predominantly uses the language of legal dispute—"How then can I contend with God? / Can I find the words to dispute God?" (verse 14)—while chapter 10 speaks in terms of divine creativity.

☐ Chapter 9

1 Job answered:

2 "I know indeed that it is so.
But how can one be righteous before God?
3 Even if one argued with God
one could not answer once in a thousand.
4 Heart of wisdom, vastly powerful,
who is hardened against God and avoids harm?
5 One who moves mountains before you know it,
overturning them angrily,
6 one who shakes Earth loose—
her pillars tremble—
7 who tells the sun, 'Don't shine,'
seals up the stars—
8 all alone God laid out the heavens,
trod down the sea—
9 who made Great Bear, Orion,
the Pleiades, the South Wind's chambers,
10 one who does great deeds beyond understanding,
wonders unnumbered.

11 "God moves past, but I do not see God;
God goes on and I do not perceive God.
12 God takes—who can stop God?
Who can say, 'What are you doing?'

(continued on page 45)

1 Rahab was the chaos monster subdued by God in creation (see Psalm 89:10, "You crushed Rahab," and Isaiah 51:9, "Was it not you who cut Rahab in pieces?").

2 Even when wicked people prosper by becoming owners of property, God does not intervene—and not only that, God causes the human judges, who are supposed to carry out the divine mandates of justice, to turn a blind eye. And if it is not God who blinds the judges to injustice, then who is it?

13 No heavenly being can hold off God's anger—
even Rahab's[1] minions take cover from God.
14 How then can I contend with God?
Can I find the words to dispute God?
15 Even were I righteous, I could not answer,
but would beg mercy from my judge.
16 If I called, and God answered me,
I don't believe God would listen to me.
17 God would crush me for no more than a whisper,
multiply my injuries for no reason.
18 God would not let me catch my breath,
but would stuff me with bitterness.
19 For power, God is strong!
For justice, who can bring God in?

20 "Even were I righteous, my own mouth condemns me.
Were I blameless, God would call me guilty.
21 I am blameless.
I am not concerned for myself.
I loathe my life.
22 It's all one: so I say.
God destroys blameless and wicked both.
23 When a scourge kills suddenly
God mocks innocent despair.
24 The land falls to wicked hands,
God covers the judges' faces—
if not God, who?[2]

(*continued on page 47*)

3 A series of images of unimpeded movement: a runner, a reed boat carried on the current, and a stooping (diving) eagle.

4 Verses 28–31 address God directly as "you."

25 "My days go more quickly[3] than a runner;
they race past with no glimpse of good;
26 they float past like reed boats;
just as an eagle stoops for prey.
27 Were I to say, 'I forget my trouble,
I will change my face and smile,'
28 I still dread my suffering;
I know you[4] will not find me innocent.
29 I am already guilty—
why struggle uselessly?
30 If I washed myself with soap,
cleansed my hands with lye,
31 You would plunge me into the cesspool,
my very clothes would abhor me.

32 "God is not one like me that I might confront God,
that we might meet in court.
33 Would that there were an arbiter between us
to put a hand on both
34 that God might remove God's rod from me
so that God's terrors would not dismay me.
35 Then I would speak. Then I would not fear God.
But it is not so with me."

1 The imagery here is based on an ancient understanding of how human beings (or indeed any mammals born from a womb) are formed. It depends on an analogy drawn from planting seed in a field. The "milky fluid" is the male ejaculate, seen as containing the "seed" of the human being. It is deposited in the womb, the medium for its growth (like soil for a seed), where it coagulates (as cheese curdles from milk) and draws on the blood and nutrients available there (it was believed that the womb filled with blood during gestation, since the female did not menstruate while pregnant and the birth, when it occurred, was accompanied with bloody fluid). The coagulation continues with greater complexity, covering the gestating being with skin and flesh and forming its bones and tendons. Job's point is that God oversees and carries out this process, so why waste the life that has been so laboriously created?

☐ Chapter 10

1 "My soul loathes my life;
I will complain freely,
out of my soul's bitterness will I speak.
2 I will say to God, 'Do not condemn me.
Tell me what you charge me with!'

3 "Is it good to you that you oppress,
that you disdain the work of your hands,
while you smile on the plots of the wicked?
4 Do you have eyes of flesh?
Do you indeed see as mortals see?
5 Are your days like those of mortals,
your years as human years—
6 so that you search out my fault,
seek out my sin?

7 "You know I am not guilty,
but no one delivers me from your hand.
8 Your hands formed and made me—
do you now turn and destroy me?
9 Remember! You made me from clay—
and will you turn me back to dust?
10 Did you not pour me out, a milky fluid,
clot me like cheese—
11 clothe me with skin and flesh—
knit my bones and sinews?[1]

(continued on page 51)

49

2 Verses 20–22 are reminiscent of two psalms. First Job evokes Psalm 39:12–13: "I am your [God's] passing guest…. Turn your gaze away from me, that I may smile again, before I depart and am no more." Then he recalls Psalm 139:11–12, but he reverses the idea: "If I say, 'Surely the darkness shall cover me, and the light around me become night,' even the darkness is not dark to you; the night is as bright as the day, for darkness is as light to you." Job's phrase "The very light is darkness" (verse 22) is echoed in Milton's *Paradise Lost* (1.63): "No light, but rather darkness visible." This is the poem's way of evoking the despair of a life of suffering that will end only in the darkness of death.

12 "Life and mercy you granted to me,
And your providence cared for my spirit,
13 but these things you hid in your heart;
I know what was in you:
14 If I sinned, you were watching me;
you would not let my guilt go unpunished.
15 If I am culpable—woe is me!
If I am innocent, I cannot raise my head—
filled with shame!
You see my affliction!

16 "In your height you stalk me like a lion,
once more showing great power against me.
17 Again you are hostile to me;
your anger against me grows;
your host comes in waves upon me.

18 "Why bring me from the womb?
Would that I had died unseen
19 as if I had never been,
borne from the womb to the grave.
20 My days are few—are they not over?
Turn from me! Give me a moment's joy!
21 Before I go and do not return,
to the land of gloom, of dark shadow,
22 of darkness like night,
of dark shadow, disarray,
the very light is darkness."**2**

In Zophar's first speech, he mockingly replies to Job by pointing out that God is far superior to human beings, so far above us as to be utterly beyond human understanding. In fact, Job himself has never denied this and has said so explicitly. If Job will only repent of his error, Zophar continues, and reach out to God, he will find that he has left his troubles behind and his life will be one of light and safety, while the lives of the wicked will end in failure.

☐ Chapter 11

1 Zophar the Naamathite answered:
  2 "Many words—but no answer?
  Is this speechifier justified?
  3 Will your empty talk silence others?
  Will you mock without rebuke?
  4 You say, 'My belief is pure,
  I am clean in your eyes.'

  5 "May God bring someone to speak,
  may God open that one's lips against you,
  6 so that God might show you hidden wisdom—
  true understanding has two sides—
  know that God has even forgotten some of your guilt.

  7 "Can you plumb God's depths?
  Reach to the limits of the Mighty One?
  8 They are higher than the heavens—what can you do?
  Deeper than the Pit—what can you know?
  9 They extend longer than Earth,
  under the Sea.
  10 If God comes to imprison,
  or passes sentence, who can resist God?
  11 For indeed God knows who is false;
  when God sees evil, does God not notice?

(continued on page 55)

1 A statement of impossibilities, as is the common saying today, "When pigs fly...."

12 "One of no wits will grow wise
when a wild donkey is born tame.[1]
13 If you yourself would dedicate your heart,
stretch out your hand to God—
14 if you put aside the guilt in your hand
and do not allow evil within your tent—
15 then indeed you will raise your face unashamed,
you will stand firm and fearless.

16 "Indeed you would then forget trouble,
remembering it as water gone by.
17 Life would be more than noontime bright,
darkness become like the morning.
18 You would be safe because there is hope,
look about and rest in safety.
19 You will lie down with none to make you afraid,
many will seek your favor.
20 The eyes of the wicked will droop,
escape will fail them,
their hope will be their last gasp."

[✒] Job's lengthy speech marks the conclusion of the first cycle of this dialogue. It is more than a response to Zophar, taking in as it does themes from the preceding chapters. Job begins by agreeing that God's wisdom and might are far above his, but he then turns the tables on his friends by pointing out that, as God is so powerful and mighty, God must have brought about Job's suffering, and indeed the suffering of every living being. If great and powerful people are cast down, if nations and empires collapse, God is behind it all. But, Job goes on to say, in spite of knowing this, he still wishes to make his case before God. He wants to do this above all because the case that the friends are making is not good enough, and God would not agree to have them speak on his behalf. In fact, God would be greatly displeased if God were to hear their case and realize that they were distorting the truth in God's defense. (This point is powerfully recalled in 42:7–8.)

Instead, Job proposes that his friends simply remain silent and let him speak, whatever consequences may ensue. He will make his case as long as God will let him and not silence him either by overcoming him physically or by overpowering his spirit with the divine majesty. Then Job demands to be told what wrong he has done and accuses God of hiding and of treating Job—who is to God as a dried leaf or the waste from threshed grain is to a human being—as God's enemy. Human beings, Job points out, are ephemeral creatures, their lives brief and soon extinguished. Trees can sprout again, but a human being, once dead, is dead for good. Furthermore, Job insists, even God will someday regret the waste of Job's life, for God's actions mean that Job will be overcome and gone forever, gone as permanently as fallen mountains and worn-away stones. After he is gone, the doings of his descendants, whether good or bad, will be nothing to him—he will not know of anything but his own suffering that will end in death.

☐ Chapter 12

1 Job answered:
2 "No doubt you are people of note,
and wisdom will die when you do.
3 But I, just as much as you, have a mind—
I am not less than you—
so who is it who does not know all this?

4 "I am a mockery to any neighbor—
though when I called, God answered—
a mockery though downright upright.
5 Those at ease have contempt for disaster,
the fate of those whose foot slips.
6 Marauders' tents are safe—
God-provokers are secure—
those whose God is their own might.
7 But ask the beasts—they will teach you;
birds of the air will tell you;
8 speak to Earth—she will teach you;
fish of the sea will instruct you.
9 Which one of all these does not know
that the LORD's hand did this?

10 "In God's hand is every life-soul,
The breath of all human flesh.
11 Does not the ear test words
as the palate tastes food?

(continued on page 59)

1   Since those taken captive in wars of conquest, especially conquered rulers, were often paraded by their conquerors without the garments that denoted their status, or even naked, this seems to refer to those who are brought low in war.

12 Is wisdom among the aged,
understanding among those with length of days?
13 With God there is wisdom, strength,
with God counsel, understanding.

14 "Look! God tears down, and it cannot be rebuilt;
God imprisons someone, and does not set free.
15 Look! God holds back waters and there is drought;
God looses them, they overwhelm the earth.
16 His are power, victory,
his the deceiver and the deceived.
17 God leads counselors away stripped,
makes fools of judges;
18 removes the belts from kings,
leaving their loins in cloth;
19 God brings priests stripped
and overthrows the prominent.[1]
20 God silences the trusted ones,
banishes the reason of the elders,
21 pours contempt on the noble,
disrobes the powerful—
22 bringing out deep things from the dark,
bringing dark shadows to light.

23 "God makes nations great, and ruins them,
enlarges nations and scatters them,
24 deprives the rulers of intelligence,
sends them meandering in pathless waste.
25 They grope in unlighted dark;
God makes them reel like drunks."

1 Job's questions here (verses 7–11) argue that lying, or even shading the truth, when one is trying to defend God's actions would not be acceptable to God.

☐ Chapter 13

1 "Look! My eye has seen all of it,
my ear has heard and understood it.
2 I know what you know;
I am not your inferior.
3 But I would speak to the Mighty One,
I wish to argue my case with God.

4 "You, however, smear me with slander;
useless physicians, all of you!
5 Better to be silent!
For you, that would be wise.
6 Listen now! Here is my argument;
pay attention to the plea of my lips.
7 Are you speaking evil[1] for God's sake?
For God you are speaking with guile?
8 Are you partial in God's presence?
Arguing God's case, are you?
9 Would it be good if God examined you?
Could you deceive God as you would deceive a man?
10 Surely God would rebuke you
if secretly, in God's presence, you were partial.
11 Would not awe of God astound you?
Dread of God overcome you?
12 Your commonplaces are proverbs of ash;
your defenses are nothing but clay.

13 "Be quiet! Let me speak!
Then whatever comes can come.

(continued on page 63)

2 The traditional translation of this verse—"Though he slay me, yet will I trust in him; but I will maintain mine own ways before him" (King James Version)—is an effort to make sense of a somewhat unusual phrasing in the Hebrew text: it reads literally something like "I hope for him" or "I trust to him." If, however, the word *lo(w)* (meaning "to or for him [God]") is spelled differently, becoming the Hebrew word for "not" (*lo'*), then the translation here makes more sense—"I have no hope" or "I'm in a hopeless situation."

3 Changed from the Hebrew, which has this in the third person ("He disintegrates").

14 I'm laying my flesh on the line,
putting my life out there in my hand.
15 God might slay me—I have no hope—
but I will defend my actions to God's face!**2**
16 It might even be what saves me
since no one profane would come to face God.

17 "You must listen to my words!
Let my speech into your ears.
18 See! I have my judgment ready—
I know I am in the right!
19 Who would bring a charge against me?
If any did, I would shut up and die.
20 Just two things do not do to me:
then I will not hide from your face.
21 Keep your hand far from me,
and don't terrify me with your dread.
22 Call me! I will certainly respond—
or—let me speak, and then you reply.
23 How great are my faults and sins?
Show me my offense and sin!
24 Why do you hide your face,
and think I am your enemy?
25 Will you harass a blowing leaf?
Will you chase dry chaff?
26 You write bitterly against me,
make me answerable for my youthful faults.
27 You put my feet in shackles;
you watch everywhere I go
by marking the soles of my feet.
28 I disintegrate**3** like something rotten,
like moth-eaten cloth."

1 Apparently a later interpolation by a religious copyist.

2 This verse may be another echo of Psalm 39:13 (Hebrew verse 14), in which the psalmist addresses God: "Turn your gaze away from me, that I may smile again, before I depart and am no more." See comments on 7:16,19; 10:20.

☐ Chapter 14

1 "One born of woman
has few days and much trouble:
2 shoots up like a flower, withers,
vanishes like a shadow, does not last.
3 Is this what you have your eye on?
Would you bring me into your judgment?
4 *[Who can give pure for impure? No one.]*[1]
5 One's days are numbered,
the tally of months is yours,
you set the bounds, one cannot exceed them.

6 "Look away from him—leave him alone—
so he can enjoy his time of service.[2]
7 For a tree, at least, there is hope:
if it is cut down, new shoots will sprout and will not fail;
8 though its roots may age in the earth,
its stump die in the soil,
9 it will smell water and sprout,
sending out shoots like a young plant.
10 But any human being who dies is felled;
one draws a last breath and is no more.

(continued on page 67)

3 That is, you would watch over me, but in order to care for me, not in order to catch me in wrongdoing.

4 These images of change under relentless pressure—moving from the slowest (leveling of mountains) to the quickest (soil erosion from flooding)—express Job's sense of the divine assault on human hope.

11 "The waters leave a sea,
a river dries up, withers,
12 so one lies down and does not get up again;
until the heavens are no more they do not awake;
they are not shaken from their sleep.
13 Would you grant me concealment in the Pit,
hide me until your wrath had passed?
Then you would set a time and remember me.

14 "If one dies, will he live again?
All the days of my weary work I endure
until the new sprouting come.
15 You call—I, I would answer—
and you would yearn for your hand's work.
16 Indeed then you would count my steps,
but not tally my sin.[3]
17 My offenses would be sealed up;
you would cover over my wrongdoing.

18 "But a mountain breaks down,
a rock shifts in place,
19 water wears stone away,
rushing streams wash down the earth's soil—
so do you ruin anyone's hope.[4]
20 You overpower him; he is gone forever.
You alter his face's expression and send him off.
21 His sons are honored—he does not know it;
they fall in disgrace—he does not see it.
22 Only his own flesh pains him;
Only for his own being does he mourn."

The Second Dialogue Cycle

Eliphaz's second speech begins the second dialogue cycle of the poem (chapters 15–21). He starts by accusing Job of undermining the importance of religious awe and, more specifically, of claiming a greater knowledge of God's inner counsels and of the dawn of creation than he can possibly have. Eliphaz then changes course by appealing to tradition and the teaching of wise elders: no human being can claim purity, and since God does not trust even the heavenly beings, who are holiest and closest to God, how much less would God trust a human being, immersed in evil? From this he moves to a description of the life of a wicked person, fearful, with enemies at every turn. But, says Eliphaz, the seeming prosperity of such an individual will not last; he will perish prematurely, like unripe grapes on the vine or an olive tree that loses its blossoms before it can produce olives.

Literally, "that prompts your mouth."

☐ Chapter 15

1 Eliphaz the Temanite replied:
2 "Would one who is wise answer with wind,
or fill his belly with the desert air?
3 Would he argue uselessly with words,
with worthless speeches?
4 But you! You undercut any awe,
any devotion to God.
5 It's your guilt making you talk like this,[1]
choosing the speech of cleverness.
6 And your own mouth condemns you, not I;
your very lips witness against you.

7 "Are you the first-born of humankind?
Born before the hills?
8 Do you have the inside track for God's advisors?
Are you the only one with wisdom?
9 What do you know that we don't?
What understanding have you that we haven't?
10 The gray-haired, the elders are with us;
they are older than your father.
11 God's solace is not enough for you?
nor are words gently spoken?
12 Why are you so carried away,
and why flash your eyes?
13 So you can let out your anger against God,
spewing words from your mouth?

(continued on page 73)

71

2 This is not a general comment about women, but a definition of a human being—someone with a physical mother.

3 This verse is apparently an interpolation.

4 Literally, "with neck," meaning stiff-necked.

14 "What human being could be pure?
How can one who is birthed from woman be righteous?**2**
15 If even in God's own holy ones God does not trust,
if even the heavens are not pure in God's eyes,
16 how would God view one vile, corrupt,
the human being, slurping evil like water?

17 "I will tell you—listen to me!—
let me explain what I have seen,
18 what the wise have said,
their fathers had not hidden—
19 *[to them only was given the land,
no foreigner traveled in their midst]***3**—
20 All the wicked one's days are torment;
few the tally of years for the pitiless.
21 Frightful things sound in his ears;
he is at peace, and despoilers attack him.
22 He cannot count on turning from darkness;
he is meant for the sword.
23 He wanders, food for vultures—
he knows the day of darkness impends.
24 Dread terrifies him,
anguish overwhelms him,
like a king ready to attack,
25 because he shook his fist at God,
strutted his stuff against the Mighty One.
26 He attacks him stubbornly,**4**
with thick-backed shield.

(continued on page 75)

5 A symbol of arrogance.

6 An interpolation.

27 "Even if he greases his face with fat—⁵
if his midsection bulges with it—
28 he will yet dwell in ruined cities,
abandoned houses,
tumbledown homes.
29 He will not be rich, his wealth will not last,
his possessions will not overspread the land,
30 he will not escape the dark;
the flame will wither his shoots;
he will be carried away by the breath of his mouth.
31 *[Let him not trust in emptiness, deceiving himself;
it is emptiness.]*⁶

32 "When it is not yet his day, it comes due;
his branch will not flourish.
33 like the vine, stripped of unripe grapes,
like the olive tree that shed its blossoms.
34 For the godless grasp is barren;
fire will consume the tents of those who bribe;
35 they conceive woe, bear evil,
their womb gestates deceit."

⚶ Job denounces his "comforters" for offering no solace, but only empty speech. He claims that he himself would offer encouragement if they were in his place and he in theirs. He has no comfort, however, either in speaking or remaining silent. Job then denounces God, alternating in his distress between talking about God in the third person and crying out a lament to God directly. Job's description of his sufferings casts them in a physical form, but these images are not to be taken literally; they use the language of bodily injury to express the anguish of mental and emotional distress. In a direct emotional, rhetorical appeal (technically called an apostrophe), Job calls on the earth not to hide his blood, but to show the evidence, so that his vindicator—the ally or advocate who will support him and plead on his behalf—can strengthen his appeal.

Job nonetheless sees himself as heading to death, his life as effectively over. His friends won't stand up for him, and in fact they denounce him. He has nothing to look forward to but to rest in the grave, accompanied by worms, but not by hope.

1 Literally, "a lot," "plenty," "many things."

2 Job's agitation is shown in verses 7–9 as he switches between second and third person address, first talking *about* God and then speaking directly *to* God.

3 Literally, "his eyes pierce me."

☐ Chapter 16

1 Job replied:
  2 "I have heard more than enough[1] of this!
  You are all miserable comforters!
  3 Any end to these windy speeches?
  What sickness keeps you arguing?
  4 I, even I, could talk like you,
  if you were in my place;
  I could speak eloquently against you,
  and shake my head at you.

  5 "But I would speak to encourage you,
  soothe you with the comfort of my lips.
  6 But if I speak, my distress has no relief;
  if I cease it does not leave me.

  7 "Surely God has now worn me down—
  You destroyed my whole household![2]
  8 you grabbed me!—it rises against me,
  my leanness shows in my face.
  9 God's anger rips, assaults me;
  God gnashes God's teeth at me;
  my enemy looks right through me.[3]

(continued on page 79)

4   Onlookers.

5   Literally, "kidneys."

6   Like a wounded animal.

7   With weeping; or perhaps "are dark," that is, showing fatigue, such as circles under the eyes.

10 "They**4** stare open-mouthed;
they sneer; they smack my cheeks;
they unite against me.
11 God turned me over to an evil one;
God threw me into the hands of the wicked.
12 I was peaceful and God smashed me;
God clutched me by the neck and crushed me;
God made me God's target—
13 God's archers surrounded me—
God has no pity as God stabs my vitals;**5**
God spills my bile on the ground.
14 God breaks out at me over and over,
charges at me like a warrior.

15 "I have sewn sackcloth over my skin;
I have bowed my horn to the dust;**6**
16 my face is reddened with weeping;
my eyes grow dim**7**
17 but my hands hold no violence,
and my prayer is pure.

18 "O Earth! Do not hide my blood!
Do not bury my cry!
19 See! Even now is my witness in heaven,
my advocate on high,
20 my mediator is my friend,
and to God my eye weeps tears,
21 pleading with God on one's behalf,
as one does for a friend.
22 The years go past,
and I will go on the way of no return."

1 Or "those who mock are around me."

2 Literally, "comparison," "proverb."

3 Verses 8–9 are generally thought to have been inserted later, since they contradict what Job has been saying.

☐ Chapter 17

1 "My spirit is broken;
my days are over;
the grave is for me.
2 Surely the underworld is around me,**1**
my eye rests on the death-pit.
3 Take my pledge to yourself!
Who else will stand security for me?
4 Since you have shut their hearts to understanding,
you cannot let them be exalted.

5 "If for a reward one denounces a friend,
that one's children will go blind.
6 God has made me the standard cliché,**2**
the one in whose face they spit.
7 My eyes dim with grief,
my body grows shadowy."

8 *[The upright are astonished,*
the innocent roused up against the profane;
9 *but the righteous one holds to his way,*
*and those with clean hands grow in strength.]***3**

(continued on page 83)

4   Job sees his closest relations as being the dissolution of death; see also Psalm 88:18 (Hebrew verse 19): "You [God] took far from me my loved ones, my companions; my only friend is darkness" (author's translation).

10 "But all of you! Come back! Come on!
I won't find a wise man among you.
11 My days have passed on,
my plans, my heart's desires, splintered.
12 They turn night into day,
light is near in the face of darkness.
13 If I hope for home in the Pit,
spread out my bed in the dark,
14 call corruption my father,
the worm my mother or my sister,⁴
15 then where is my hope?
Who can see my hope?
16 Will it go with me to the open Pit?
Will we descend together to the dust?"

[✍] In his second speech, Bildad briefly denounces Job as having no sense himself while accusing others of folly. He then returns to the favored theme of the friends: Whatever may be the case in the short run, in the long run the wicked have short, insecure lives. After their deaths, their memory is blotted out, they leave no descendants, and even the places in which they once dwelled are cursed.

□ Chapter 18

1 Bildad the Shuhite replied:
    2 "How much longer will you set snares in speech?
    Show some sense! Then we can talk.
    3 Why are we like cattle,
    dullards, in your view?
    4 You!—someone who tears himself with anger.
    Is the earth deserted for your sake?
    Is a rock displaced?

    5 "The wicked one's lamp is snuffed;
    his fiery flame burns out.
    6 The light in his tent grows dim;
    his nearby lamp goes out.
    7 His pace falters ... halts;
    his own plots trip him.
    8 He is pushed feet-first into the net;
    he stumbles in the mesh.
    9 The trap grabs his heel;
    the snare grips him.
    10 His noose lies concealed on the ground,
    his trap in the path.
    11 All around, terrors shake him,
    harry, harrow his steps.
    12 Calamity hungers for him,
    disaster awaits his fall.

(continued on page 87)

85

1   This refers to death.

13 "The two-fisted skin eater,
first-born Death, devours him.
14 He is yanked from his tent, from safety,
and marched to the Terror-king.[1]
15 Fire dwells in his tent,
burning sulfur falls where he lives.
16 Below, his roots dry up;
above, his branch withers.
17 Any memory of him perishes from the earth;
his name is unknown throughout the land.
18 Hurried from light to darkness,
driven from the world,
19 no offspring for him, no descendants among his kin,
no survivor where he once lived—
20 his fate appalls those in the west,
horror seizes those in the east—
21 surely these were abodes where an evil man lived,
a place of one who didn't know God."

🔖 In his response, Job, in effect, abandons any argument aimed at self-justification and instead takes his friends to task for their lack of sympathy with his condition. He then turns to God's acts, which, he claims, have completely destroyed his life. His relatives are abandoning him, his servants refuse to obey him, his immediate family avoids his physical stench. He endures the scorn of young children and mistreatment by his friends. In short, Job is wasting away, and he turns once again to his friends for sympathy and pity. He wishes that his story could be written down "with a tool of iron" (verse 24) and his complaint preserved on record. Yet Job also expresses his faith that ultimately there will be justice—that some being will stand by him and bring him face-to-face with God.

□ Chapter 19

1 Job answered:
    2 "How long will you torture me?
    Crush me with words?
    3 You've rebuked me ten times,
    and attacked me shamelessly.
    4 If, in fact, I've gone astray,
    is it my mistake?

    5 "If you would put yourselves above me,
    use my shame against me,
    6 then know this: God undid me,
    drew God's net around me.
    7 I cry, 'Violence!'—no response!
    I call, 'Help!'—no justice!
    8 God blocks my way—I can't get through;
    God casts darkness on my path.
    9 God has stripped honor from me,
    taken the crown from my head.
    10 God has completely demolished me; I'm undone.
    God uproots my hope like a tree.
    11 God's anger flares against me;
    God includes me among God's enemies.
    12 God's forces march against me;
    they besiege me;
    they are camped around my tent.

(continued on page 91)

1   The traditional rendering "I have escaped by the skin of my teeth" does not convey what Job is saying. He seems to mean, "My actual skin is being destroyed, and my bones are sticking through it; it's as if I have no skin other than the skin on my teeth" (which is highly ironic, since teeth do not have any skin).

13 "My relatives have given up on me;
my friends God turns into strangers.
14 My kin and my close friends have left me,
those who lived with me have forgotten me.
15 My servant-girls see me as a stranger,
as an alien in their eyes.
16 I call my servant—no answer!
Even when I beg!
17 My breath offends my wife,
I stink to my own offspring.
18 Even small boys treat me scornfully;
when I go out, they make fun of me.
19 My close friends despise me;
those I love turn against me.
20 My bones stick out through my flesh;
the only skin I have is on my teeth.[1]

21 "For pity's sake, my friends, pity me!
God's hand has hit me hard.
22 Why do you, like God, chase me down?
Haven't you gotten enough of my flesh?
23 Would that my words were written!—
that they were inscribed on a scroll!—
24 with a tool of iron, and lead,
engraved in stone forever.

(continued on page 93)

2 This figure of the vindicator, or redeemer, is interpreted in classical Christian exegesis as referring to Jesus Christ, who will vindicate (or redeem) the sinner. But the actual meaning of the verse is more like Job's final hope: "I know that there is someone who will stand up for me and help me present my case for justice with God." The vindicator was originally a member of the extended family who was responsible for getting someone out of debt or other trouble—the "redeemer" who would pay to get the person out of the clutches of creditors or even released from slavery. In its extended sense, the word also refers to one who acts as an advocate or ally in a legal argument, which is what Job has said all along that he wants to have.

For centuries Christian interpreters have read Job as an example of a human being who is redeemed by Jesus Christ. This is reflected in the traditional translation, "I know that my Redeemer liveth," perhaps best known from the final section of Handel's *Messiah*. According to this point of view, Job is able to look down the centuries and foresee the future rescue of sinful humanity by a heavenly being who will be the defender and advocate for sinners when they appear before the judgment throne of God. The translation offered here, however, gives a version of this passage that differs from the traditional Christian interpretation.

25 "I know my vindicator[2] lives
and in the end will stand upon the dust—
26 even when my skin has perished,
my very flesh, I shall see God—
27 I, even I, will see—
my eyes, no other—
my heart burns and yearns!

28 "If you say, 'How might we harry him?'—
since trouble's root nestles within me—
29 then beware! The sword of wrath,
the sword will punish,
so that you will know judgment!"

In his second speech, Zophar returns to the earlier argument, claiming that in fact the wicked never prosper. Even if they seem to be doing well, their apparent prosperity is momentary: soon they will meet their downfall, die, and be gone beyond recall and beyond memory. Furthermore, if the rich man's wealth was gotten by fraud, his children will have to give it up to pay back those whom he cheated. And although the wicked man will savor his wealth at first, most likely it will ultimately become to him as poison, forcing him to disgorge all his gains. A wicked man who can never amass enough, never be satisfied with the food or the houses he has, will get a belly-full from God— pierced through with a blade or an arrow. All his guilty deeds will be revealed, and all of the wealth he has put together will be washed away in God's wrath.

☐ Chapter 20

1 Zophar the Naamathite replied:
  2 "My distressed thoughts impel me to speak
  because of my agitation.
  3 To my own dishonor I have listened to this rebuke,
  and my own discernment of spirit gives me an answer.

  4 "You know this from ages past,
  since human beings took their place on earth—
  5 that the glee of the wicked is fleeting,
  the joy of the impious momentary.
  6 His pride may reach toward heaven,
  his head may touch the cloud;
  7 but he will die like his own dung, utterly,
  and any who saw him will ask, 'Where is he?'
  8 He has flitted off like a dream, nowhere found,
  dispersed like a night-vision.
  9 The eye sees him—then never does again;
  no more will his place regard him.
  10 His children must recompense the poor;
  his very hands must hand over his wealth.
  11 His bones, the strength of youth,
  lie along with him in the dust.

  12 "Even if evil lies sweet in his mouth,
  lurks under his tongue—
  13 he saves and savors, won't let it go,
  keeps it between tongue and palate—
  14 nonetheless the food in his gut will turn,
  vile as vipers' venom inside him.

(continued on page 97)

1 | Fire blazing so fiercely that it does not need wind in order to burn everything in its path.

2 | As the wicked one's possessions—and along with them his social status—are swept away in the flood of God's wrath, the true character of his wickedness will appear, and his guilt will be exposed.

15 He will spew out the riches he swallowed;
God will force his belly to vomit.
16 Vipers' venom he'll suck;
fangs of asp will slay him.

17 "He will not savor oil in streams,
nor rivulets of honey and cream.
18 He will not eat, but give back, his produce;
he will not enjoy the wealth he traded to obtain,
19 because he crushed and despoiled the poor—
grabbed houses and lands he never worked for.
20 His lust for possession never slackened,
his treasure never sated him,
21 there's nothing left for him to grab—
so his goods will not last.

22 "At his height of wealth disaster strikes,
misery comes upon him in full force.
23 He'll have his belly full, all right—
God will blast him with blazing anger,
pelt him with shattering blows!
24 He may flee from the iron blade,
but the bronze arrow will pierce him,
25 the shaft through and out the back,
the point glittering from his liver.
Terror will overcome him,
26 utter darkness lie in wait for his treasures,
fire unfanned consume him,[1]
lap up what's left in his tent.
27 Heaven will bare his guilt,
Earth arise against him.
28 His goods, his house, shall wash away,[2]
flooded on the day of wrath.
29 This is God's fate for the wicked,
the inheritance that God appoints."

In direct contradiction to what Zophar has just said, Job maintains in his response that in fact the wicked do prosper and never get called to account. Even when they disregard God, they are not punished. And as for Zophar's point that even if a wicked man is not brought to justice, his children must pay, Job is withering in his rebuttal. First he claims that effective justice should fall on the perpetrator—"Better God pay the one who does it—then he'd know!" (verse 19)—and then points out that the persecutor won't care what happens after he's dead, so what difference does punishing his children make? And even if someone suffers in this life, Job argues, it doesn't ultimately matter. The fact is that all die, and all go to the earth together, good and bad, those who prosper and those who suffer. And just look at the burials of the wealthy! No matter what they did to become rich, "unnumbered crowds" (verse 33) will follow the body to the grave, where it is buried in comfort.

☐ Chapter 21

1 Then Job replied:
2 "Just listen! Will you listen to my words?
That would be consolation enough!
3 Bear with me! I will speak—
once I have spoken, go ahead and mock.

4 "Am I complaining to a human being?
Why shouldn't I be impatient?
5 Look at me! Astounding!
Clap your hand over your mouth!

6 "If ever I think of this, I sink in terror;
trembling strikes my flesh.
7 Why do the wicked still live?
Grow old, and grow in strength?
8 Their offspring secure,
their progeny all about them.
9 Their peaceful homes have no fear,
God's punishment never upon them.
10 His bull sires every time;
his cow calves without mishap.
11 They have flocks of infants,
and these little ones dance around.
12 They sing to tambourine and harp,
play to the voice of the flute.

(continued on page 101)

1 Literally, "and in an instant go down to *Sheol.*"

2 This seems to be an insertion by another editor, trying to mitigate the force of Job's cynicism by pointing out that no one controls his own well-being.

13 They pass their time in prosperity
and slip easily into death.**1**
14 Though they say to God, 'Let us be!
We don't need to know your ways.
15 Who is the Mighty One—are we supposed to serve God?
What is the use of our prayers to God?'"

16 *[Look! Their well-being is not under their control;*
*the views of the wicked are far from mine.]***2**

17 "How often, really, is a wicked one's lamp snuffed out?
Or does ruin befall them?
Or does God apportion their fate in God's anger?
18 Are they straws in the wind?
chaff swept off in a gale?
19 God stores up punishment for the children? Truly?
Better God pay the one who does it—then he'd know!
20 Let his own eyes see his ruin!
Let him drink the Mighty One's wrath himself!
21 What concern of his is his family after he's gone—
when his time is up?

22 "Can he teach God knowledge?
Judge those on high?
23 One may die vigorous to the end,
satisfied, secure, calm,
24 filled with nourishment,
bones rich in marrow;
25 another may die bitter in soul,
never knowing any goodness.
26 Yet there they lie, together, in the dust,
worms upon them.

(continued on page 103)

3   This is the most fertile soil. Even in death, Job says, the wicked claim the best land.

27 "Look! I know what you're thinking,
how you plot to do me wrong.
28 You say, 'Where is the great one's house?
Where are the tents of the wicked?'
29 Have you not spoken with travelers,
paid any attention to their tales?
30 The evil escape the day of ruin,
are delivered from the day of wrath.
31 Who condemns his behavior to his face?
Who will repay him for what he has done?
32 He is brought to the grave;
the tomb watches over him.
33 How sweet to him is the valley-earth!³
All the folk follow him,
unnumbered crowds go before him.
34 Why then console me with empty breath?
Your answers are lies!"

The Third
Dialogue Cycle

In his third speech, Eliphaz returns to his earlier charge that Job has committed—or must have committed—some sin or wrongdoing to deserve his suffering. What's more, Job's protestations of righteousness shouldn't make any difference because human righteousness makes no difference to God. Here Eliphaz depicts Job as an evildoer suddenly frightened of the darkness in which he finds himself, trying to buck up his courage by saying that God is far away and cannot possibly see what he is doing. But, says Eliphaz to Job, if you in fact turn to God, accept God's teaching, return your wealth to its source (perhaps this is an exhortation to give it back to the oppressed), and take God for your wealth, you will then be blessed indeed. In fact you will be so blessed that even your prayers for the guilty will be efficacious, and God will save them simply because it is Job—repentant Job!—who is praying for them. (The true irony of this will be revealed in 42:8–9.)

1 A reference (Exodus 22:25–26; Deuteronomy 24:10–13) to the prohibition of taking, as pledge for a loan, a poor man's only outer garment, since this will leave him no protection against the cold.

☐ Chapter 22

1 Eliphaz the Temanite answered:
   2 "Can anyone be of use to God?
   Can even the wise be of use to God?
   3 What good is it to the Mighty One if you are righteous?
   What does God gain if your ways are upright?
   4 Is it your piety God's chiding you for,
   and entering judgment against you?
   5 Your evil—is it not great?
   Your guilt—is it not endless?

   6 "You have kept your kin's pledge unfairly;
   you have stripped clothes from the naked.[1]
   7 You gave the weary no drink;
   you held back bread from the hungry—
   8 even though you were strong in the land,
   an honored one upon it.
   9 You dismissed widows empty-handed;
   you broke the power of the fatherless.
   10 Thus snares surround you,
   sudden danger frightens you,
   11 it is dark—you cannot see,
   and water-floods overwhelm you.

   12 "Is not God in high heaven?
   And look! The highest stars, how lofty!
   13 But you say, 'What does God know?
   Can God judge through the murk?
   14 Clouds envelop him, God cannot see—
   God's traveling through the heavens!'

(continued on page 109)

2   Literally, "rebuilt," "restored."

3   Abandoning one's wealth is a way of giving it back to God, perhaps not literally by throwing it away but by giving it away to the needy. In either case, the exhortation is to remove it from one's own possession or control.

15 Ah, the path you ever keep,
that the worthless trod before you!—
16 those who were torn away untimely,
whose foundations the floods swept off—
17 who said to God, 'Let us alone!'
and, 'What can the Mighty One do to us?'—
18 though God well filled their houses—
may such wicked advice be far from me!

19 "The righteous see and are glad,
the innocent mock them:
20 'Surely their possessions are destroyed,
fire eats up their wealth!'

21 "Serve God now! Be at peace!
And thereby goods will come your way.
22 Take the teaching that God speaks now!
Treasure in your heart what God says.
23 If you turn to the Mighty One you will be remade.[2]
Put evildoing far from your dwelling,
24 cast your precious ore back to dust,
your Ophir-gold into rocky ravines,[3]
25 and the Mighty One will be your gold,
your finest silver.
26 Then surely, in the Mighty One you will delight,
and lift your face to God.
27 You will pray to God; God will hear you;
you will carry out your vows.
28 You will decide—it will be done!
God will shine light on your ways.
29 For those brought low you may order uplifting,
and the downcast God will save.
30 God will even let one escape who is not innocent,
who will escape because your own hands are clean."

⟨✍⟩ The text of 23:1–24:17 is clearly Job's response, but after that point the text is in serious disarray. Chapter 23 begins with Job's wishing again that he could go to God with his complaint and arguments to make good his case, but God is nowhere to be found. Nevertheless, Job again insists on his innocence and his faithfulness, though he is in awe and fear of God.

⟨1⟩ The directions in verses 8–9 can also be translated "forward," "backward," "left," and "right."

☐ Chapter 23

1 Job answered:
  2 "Even now my complaint is harsh;
  the hand lies heavy on my groaning.
  3 O that God would let me know how to find God!
  I could go to God's dwelling.
  4 I would lay my judgment before God;
  my mouth would overflow with argument.
  5 I want to know God's answers,
  and I would think over what God said to me.
  6 Would God deploy legal might against me?
  Indeed, God would bring no charges against me.
  7 Thus the upright could make God's case before God;
  I would accomplish safe delivery of justice.

  8 "But I go east—God is not there;
  west—I don't find God;
  9 north I try—don't see God;
  south—can't glimpse God.[1]
  10 But God knows where I go;
  God will test me, and I'll come out like gold.
  11 I've followed God step-by-step;
  I kept God's way with no turning aside.
  12 I have not ignored any command from God's lips;
  the words of God's mouth are dearer than bread to me.

(continued on page 113)

2   Presumably, the divine decree that Job must suffer.

13 "But God is unique—who can withstand God?
God does what God wants to do.
14 God enforces the decree[2] on me;
that, and many others with it.
15 Thus I am in terror before God;
when I think of it, I fear God.
16 God weakens my heart;
the Mighty One terrifies me.
17 O, could I recede in the face of darkness—
would thick darkness cover my face!"

[✍] Job begins by wishing that God would establish set times when the faithful can appear before God to present their cases and grievances, such as indicting the acts of the wicked in moving boundaries and stealing the flocks of the poor. He then goes on to describe the plight of those who have been unjustly treated, who are forced to live out in the open without adequate food, clothing, or shelter. They are exploited, forced to work in the vineyards, fields, and olive groves of the wealthy, yet though they are surrounded by food and drink, they have none for themselves. Others among the wicked go out at night to do their deeds of murder, robbery, or adultery.

[1] Literally, "boundary stones," moving which was a serious crime (Deuteronomy 27:17).

[2] This refers to the wicked oppressors who take the children of the poor away from them and put them into slavery because their parents cannot pay off their own debts.

☐ Chapter 24

1 "Why does the Mighty One not set such times?
Why do those who know God never have their day?
2 Some move property lines[1]
and pasture their stolen flocks.
3 An orphan's donkey they drive off,
and repossess the widow's ox as a pledge.
4 They push needy ones out of the way,
the earth's destitute are forced into hiding.
5 Look! As do wild donkeys in the wilderness,
they work at foraging for food;
the wasteland is the source of their children's bread.
6 They gather from the fields
and glean the vineyards of the wicked.
7 They lie, unclothed, in the night,
lacking covering in the cold,
8 drenched with the mountain rains,
clinging to the rocks for protection.

9 "They[2] snatch from the breast the fatherless child
and seize the infants of the poor for debt.
10 They have no clothes, so go about naked;
though they haul sheaves, they go hungry.
11 They crush olives in the press,
tread the wine-grapes, yet they thirst.

(continued on page 117)

3   Verses 18–24, expressing arguments different from those of Job in his previous speeches, are transferred to the end of Bildad's speech in chapter 25, where they fit much better.

12 "Mortal groans arise from the city;
wounded souls cry for aid;
but God brings no charge of wrongdoing.
13 Some struggle against the light;
they do not know God's ways;
they do not stay in God's paths.
14 When day is gone, the murderer arises:
he kills the poor and destitute;
he is a thief in the night.
15 The adulterer looks out for the dusk,
thinking, 'No eye will see me,'
and hiding his face.
16 They are housebreakers by night;
they shut themselves off from the day,
having nothing to do with light.
17 For them, murk is morning;
they are friends to night-terrors."

*[Verses 18–24 are transferred to Bildad's response below.]*3

25 "If not, who can show I am untrue?
bring down my words to naught?"

🖉 In the Hebrew text as it stands, Bildad's third speech is only six verses long—far shorter than any other speech. The seven verses that the current arrangement has transferred from Job's speech in chapter 24 still do not make it of equal length with other speeches, but they do make more sense in the context of Bildad's response.

1 This is the original end of Bildad's speech.

2 These inserted verses, 24:18–24, originally spoken by Job, have instead been transferred to the end of Bildad's speech. They express the argument of the friends that the wicked will not flourish forever, but God will cut them down even at the height of their power.

☐ Chapter 25

1 Bildad the Shuhite answered:
2 "Rule and awe are God's;
God sets forth peace in God's exalted realm.
3 Can anyone count God's army?
Who is there on whom God's light does not rise?
4 Then how can anyone be righteous before God?
How can one born of woman be clean?
5 If even the moon is not bright
or the stars clean in God's sight,
6 how much less so is the human being, a maggot,
and human offspring, a worm?"[1]

24:18[2] "Yet they are but froth on the water;
their land-share is cursed;
and no one goes to the vineyards.

(continued on page 121)

3 Those who have no child or husband are the most vulnerable to economic exploitation.

19 Drought and heat leach off the snow;
so does the grave to sinners.
20 The womb forgets him,
the worm devours him,
he is no longer remembered;
evil broken like a tree.
21 Victimizing the barren who never bore,
showing no kindness to the widow.[3]
22 Yet God with God's might hauls off the strong;
rooted though they be, their lives are not sure.
23 God may leave them in rest and safety,
but God's eyes are on their ways.
24 For a moment they are on top,
then are gone;
they are felled and gathered like all;
they are severed like grain-heads."

⌧ Job's response mostly consists of a confession of God's power, which is evoked through a series of poetic images. His point seems to be that if God can do so much—controlling the seas, the heavens, and everything in between—why does God not act to save the innocent and punish the wicked before they all die?

1　The chaos monster (also evoked in Isaiah 51:9).

☐ Chapter 26

1 Job answered:
 2 "How much you have helped the helpless!
 strengthened the strengthless arm!
 3 How much counsel you give to the unwise,
 how great the advice you have shown!
 4 Who helped you utter these words?
 Whose spirit came out from you?

 5 "The dead writhe in pain,
 the waters and those who live beneath,
 6 the Grave is naked before God,
 and Destruction has no covering.
 7 God spreads the north over emptiness,
 hangs the earth over nothingness,
 8 enfolds the waters in God's clouds,
 the clouds that do not burst their burden.
 9 God hides the full moon's face
 overspread with God's clouds.
 10 God draws the horizon on the water's surface,
 the boundary between light and dark.
 11 The heaven's pillars shake,
 dumbfounded at God's rebuke.
 12 God's power churns the sea,
 God's cunning cuts down Rahab.[1]
 13 The wind of God's breath clears the skies,
 God's hand pierced the slippery serpent.
 14 See! These are but the edges of God's ways;
 we hear but a weak whisper of God—
 but who could comprehend the thunder of God's power?"

✍ This chapter is rearranged to provide a third speech for Zophar (verses 8–23), followed by a brief response from Job (verses 1–7). This fills out the pattern of the third cycle and also avoids having any of the participants making an argument that contradicts what he has previously maintained.

1 Verses 8–23 of this chapter, like other passages in this section, seem out of order. In this version I have given it to Zophar, who otherwise has no speech in this third cycle and thus breaks the pattern. Zophar returns to his argument that God ultimately will overthrow the wicked. The unrighteous man will perish, and his children will not inherit the fruits of his dealings, but the innocent and righteous whom he has exploited will receive the benefit of his wealth.

2 He will not be mourned.

☐ Chapter 27

[Verses 1–7 are transferred below to answer Zophar.]

[Zophar the Naamathite said:]**¹**
  8 "What hope does the impious one have when he faces death,
  when God takes his life?
  9 Does God hear his cry
  when trouble overcomes him?
  10 Will he delight in the Mighty One,
  and constantly call on God?

  11 "I will teach you about God's hand,
  and I will not hide the Mighty One's ways.
  12 Look! You've all seen this—
  why talk utter nonsense?
  13 This is the portion the wicked one has from God,
  the inheritance the pitiless receive from the Mighty One.
  14 No matter how numerous his children, they are for the sword;
  his offspring will never have bread enough.
  15 His descendants also will be hidden in death,
  and his widows will not weep.**²**
  16 He may pile up silver like dust-mounds,
  and clothing in heaps like clay-mounds,
  17 but the righteous will eat what he has laid up,
  and the innocent will share out the silver.

(continued on page 127)

3 Verses 1–7 are Job's response. In these verses, which originally appeared as the beginning of the chapter, Job once again asserts his righteousness.

18 "The house he builds is but a moth-cocoon,
a lean-to for a watchman.
19 Rich he lies down, never so again;
his eyes open on nothing.
20 Terror floods him by day;
nightly the storm seizes him.
21 The east wind sweeps him, he's gone;
whirls him from his place,
22 hurls against him pitilessly,
as he desperately flees from its power.
23 Clap! Against him, storm-hands!
Hiss! Against him from his place!"

1**3** Job continued his speech:
2 "God's life! God withheld justice from me;
the Mighty One has embittered my soul!
3 While I have any life left,
breath of God in my nostrils,
4 my lips will speak no evil,
my tongue utter no lies.
5 I will never say you are right—far from it!
Until the day I die I will not deny my integrity.
6 I assert my righteousness—I won't abandon it!
My heart will never reproach me all my days.
7 May any enemy of me be like the wicked,
any adversary like the unjust."

[Interlude on seeking wisdom]

As noted in the introduction, this speech, though it is attributed to Job, does not fit with other parts of Job's argument (including the chapter that immediately follows). Since it is easily detached from its context, it seems better to treat this speech as a poetical interlude in which the book as a whole introduces a different perspective, which is that of the quest for wisdom in a human life. In a lengthy comparison, the poet describes the difficulty of finding gold, silver, and precious gems, digging tunnels through rock and seeking out the sources of underground rivers. If this is so, then how much more difficult it is to find true wisdom! If, the poem implicitly says, you will expend all this effort in finding precious metal, ores, and gems, what will you do to find what is even more valuable? Will you risk suffering for that treasure? Ultimately, it is God alone who knows where wisdom is, and so the surest path to wisdom is to begin by holding God in awe.

☐ Chapter 28

1 There is a source of silver,
a refinery for gold,
2 iron dug from the dust,
copper smelted from stone.
3 One banishes darkness,
probes every niche,
searching rock in blackness.
4 Far from dwellings he cuts a shaft,
to places the boot has forgotten,
far from their fellows they hang and sway.
5 Below, the earth, food-source,
is changed as by fire:
6 stones yield sapphire,
dust gives gold.
7 No hawk knows that path,
no falcon's eye can see it.
8 Majestic beasts do not pad there,
no lion has been.
9 But, human hands to the flint,
baring the mount's base,
10 digging tunnels through rock,
his eye sees all the treasure.
11 He seeks the river-springs,
bringing to light what's been hidden.

    12 But wisdom—where is it found?
    Discernment—where is its place?
13 No one knows its value;
it is not found among the living.

(continued on page 131)

1   Even the ultimate powers that end human lives are not powerful enough to know where to find wisdom: they have only heard, at best, intimations of wisdom's existence.

14 The deep says, "Not in me."
The sea says, "Not with me."
15 It cannot be bought for finest gold,
nor weighed in price with silver.
16 It cannot be bought with Ophir-gold,
with precious onyx or sapphire.
17 Gold and crystals cannot compare,
gold and jewels cannot buy it.
18 Coral, jasper? Not worth mentioning.
Wisdom is beyond rubies' price.
19 Ethiopian topaz can't compare,
purest gold can't meet the price.
      20 This wisdom—where comes it?
      Discernment—where is its place?
21 It lies hidden from all living eyes,
even concealed from birds of the air.
22 Destruction and Death[1] say,
"We have heard rumors."
23 God knows its ways,
God indeed knows its dwelling.
24 God sees to the earth's limits,
oversees all under heaven,
25 set the power of wind,
carefully measured the waters,
26 made runnels for rain,
made a path for the thunderstorm,
27 saw it, valued it,
tried it, tested it—
28 and said to human beings,
"Look! Awe of the LORD, that is wisdom!
Turning from evil, discernment!"

[End of interlude]

Job's Final Speeches

Job recalls his days of greatness, the wealth and honor he enjoyed before calamity fell upon him. He had food in abundance and was respected among the citizenry. His opinions were valued; young and old both deferred to him. He defended the oppressed, and the desperate appealed to him for justice. He avenged oppression by punishing the wicked. He thought that he would die in his own house, honored to the end.

1 The area around the main gate of a city was the place where older men would gather and render judgment in the case of (mostly civil) legal disputes.

☐ Chapter 29

1 Job resumed his saying:
  2 "Ah! Would that God would give the months that are gone,
  the days when God guarded me,
  3 when God's lamp shone about my head,
  and in God's light I walked through the dark!
  4 Ah! Would I were in my prime again,
  when God's affection was upon my house,
  5 when the Mighty One was with me,
  my children around me—
  6 when I waded through cream,
  rocks poured olive oil in streams!

  7 "I would go to the city gate,[1]
  take a seat in the public square;
  8 young men when they saw me would stand aside,
  old men would rise and stand,
  9 leaders would fall silent,
  covering their mouths with a hand,
  10 voices of great ones grew quiet,
  their tongues pressed to their palates;
  11 any who heard spoke well of me,
  any who saw commended me,
  12 because I rescued the poor who cried,
  the fatherless with no other help.

(continued on page 137)

2 With this catalog of judgments, Job clearly aligns himself as advocate and defender of the poor and oppressed.

13 "The desperate blessed me,
I made the widow's heart joyous.
14 Righteousness clothed me,
justice robed and turbaned me.
15 I was sight for the blind,
feet for the lame,
16 father to the needy,
advocate for the stranger.[2]

17 "I broke the wicked one's teeth,
snatched the victim from his jaws.
18 And I thought, 'I'll die in my own house,
my days like the sand in number,
19 my roots reaching water,
night-dews spread on my branches,
20 my glory ever fresh,
the bow in my hand always new.'

21 "They listened to me attentively,
they waited in silence for my advice.
22 After I spoke, no one said anything further,
my words falling on them.
23 They waited for me as for gentle showers,
their mouths drinking the spring rain.
24 I'd smile at them—they hardly believed it!—
they'd never reject the light of my face.
25 I chose their path; I sat as their leader;
I dwelt with them as a king with his troops:
I guided their ways."

▨ But now Job is a mockery even among the people he would formerly have had nothing to do with. The expression in verse 1, somewhat shocking to contemporary readers, reflects the social realities of a time when hierarchical arrangements were taken for granted, even though it seems to counteract Job's concern for those less fortunate than he. (Contemporary readers must remember that dogs, in the ancient world, were considered not honorable and noble companions but rather unclean beasts whose public behavior was shameful.) Presumably, these new mockers are not merely those who were formerly marginal, but those who were morally inferior and therefore not worthy of honor. It is a particularly difficult part of Job's current condition, he argues, that he is subject to their scorn. Job goes on to complain about God's treatment, causing him pain, frightening him at night, dragging him ultimately to his death. Yet, in contrast to Job's care for the less fortunate, those around him now offer him no help and no comfort.

☐ Chapter 30

1 "But now they mock me,
these younger men;
formerly I'd have refused with contempt
to allow their fathers among my sheepdogs.
2 What was the strength of their hands to me?
Vigor was gone from them.
3 Desperate, hungry, haggard,
they'd chew at the parched earth,
at night, in waste and desolation,
4 gathering sour herbs in the weeds,
shrub-roots for fire,
5 shunned by the others,
shouted at like thieves,
6 to linger in dry gullies,
in holes, among rocks,
7 baying in the bushes,
huddled under the brush,
8 worthless, unknown brood,
driven from the land.

(continued on page 141)

1 This can refer either to the physical pain of Job's illness, which keeps him tossing and turning, or the mental distress of his suffering and loss of social status; in either case, the suffering causes insomnia.

9 "Yet now they sing mockery at me;
for them I'm a taunt.
10 They detest me; they avoid me;
they won't hold back from spitting in my face.
11 God has unstrung my bow, afflicted me,
so they act without restraint to my face.
12 To my right a vicious band
attacks and snares my feet;
they build their siege-ramps toward me.
13 They ruin my roads;
they destroy me without help or hindrance.
14 They smash through the breach,
roll over the ruins.

15 "Terror overcomes me;
my dignity's blown away;
my security vanishes like a cloud.
16 My life-breath is failing;
the suffering holds me for days.
17 Night stabs me to the bone,
and grinding tortures[1] never cease.
18 God grabs my garments with power,
God pulls tight around my throat.
19 God hurls me into the muck,
treats me like trash and ashes.

(continued on page 143)

2   Both jackals and ostriches, animals of the desert, give out piercing, mournful cries.

20 "I cry out—you don't answer!
I stand—you merely look at me!
21 You turn on me pitilessly;
you hit me with your strong hand.
22 You grab me and drive me like the wind,
throw me around like the storm.
23 I know you'll bring me down to death,
to the final dwelling place of all life.
24 Does one raise a hand against the shattered one,
when in his sorrow he cries to them for help?
25 Didn't I weep for those whose days are hard?
Didn't my life grieve for the poor?
26 Yet when I looked for good, evil came;
when I hoped for light, darkness came.
27 My innards churn endlessly;
days of affliction lie before me.
28 I am darkened without the sun,
I stand among the crowds and cry for help.
29 I'm brother to jackals,
companion to the ostrich-brood.**2**
30 My skin blackens and flakes off;
my bones are heated with fever.
31 My harp mourns,
my flute wails."

∞ Job recalls his righteous behavior. He did not lust after young, unmarried women. He did not commit adultery—if he did, let his own wife be unfaithful! Job treated his servants fairly; cared for the poor, widowed, and orphaned; clothed the naked; did not worship false gods. He did not even exult over his enemies when they fell into misfortune. He provided for the homeless. He did not gather any crops that he was not entitled to or that he did not pay for. All this is part of his defense, so Job is ready to turn over his evidence and read the indictment from God.

1 Literally, "virgin."

2 Possibly a metaphor for "offspring."

3 If Job has "hung around" a neighbor's house, presumably to enter into an adulterous liaison with his wife, then may Job's wife herself commit adultery ("grind" here has sexual overtones, though conventionally it means "grind meal," that is, prepare food for someone, as a wife does for her husband).

4 The point of this description, of course, is that, like the other behaviors he has described, Job has not done this.

☐ Chapter 31

1 "I made a covenant: my eyes
would never look at an unmarried girl.**1**
2 What lot does God send from above?
What heritage does the Mighty One provide?
3 Isn't it calamity for the evil,
woe for the wrongdoers?
4 Doesn't God see my ways,
count my very steps?
5 If my steps led to lies,
my feet hurried to deceit,
6 let God weigh me in the true balance—
may God thus know my innocence.

7 "If I have stepped from the true path—
if my eyes have led my heart astray—
if my hands have even a spot of defilement—
8 then may I sow, but another eat;
may my plantings**2** be uprooted.
9 If my heart has been seduced by a woman,
or if I've hung around my neighbor's door,
10 then let my wife grind for another,
and may others enjoy her sexually.**3**
11 For that would be shamefulness,**4**
sin worthy of judgment,
12 of a fire burning to Destruction,
destroying all my harvest.

(continued on page 147)

5 Either "I could not withstand him [God]" or "I could not do any of the things I have mentioned."

13 "If I disregarded just claims from my male or female slaves,
when they complained against me,
14 what would I do when God stands before me—
when God calls, what would I answer?
15 Didn't the one who formed me in the womb form them?
Didn't God form us all the same?

16 "If I denied the needs of the poor,
or let a widow's eyes grow dim—
17 if I ate my bread alone,
not providing any for the orphan—
18 but from my youth I raised him as would a father,
from my mother's womb I guided her.
19 If I saw someone dying for lack of clothes,
a needy one with no garment,
20 if his loins would not bless me,
warmed with fleece from my sheep,
21 if I have ever raised a hand against an orphan,
when I had influence in the judgment-gate,
22 then let my arm drop off,
let it be broken at the elbow!

23 "For I dread ruin that comes from God—
God overawes me—I could not do it.⁵
24 Had I relied on gold,
on pure gold for security,
25 had I gloried in my wealth,
the riches my hands made,
26 had I looked to the radiant light,
the moon going in splendor,

(continued on page 149)

6 A gesture of homage, here seen as being idolatrous.

27 so that my heart was inwardly seduced,
and my hand kissed my mouth—**6**
28 then that would be sin worthy of judgment,
that I had betrayed the most high God.

29 "Had I rejoiced at an enemy's misfortune,
grown glad when trouble came upon him,
30 had I allowed offense from my mouth,
calling down a curse on his life,
31 had my menservants never said,
'Who hasn't had plenty of Job's meat?'—
32 no stranger slept in the street,
my door was always open to the wayfarer.
33 Had I hidden my sin, humanly speaking,
covering my guilt in the ground,
34 so fearing the crowd,
the clans' contempt,
that I never ventured outside with anyone—
35 would that someone heard me!
I've signed on the line—let the Mighty One answer!
Let God issue the indictment, this opposing counsel!
36 I'd surely wear it on my shoulder,
put it on me like a crown;
37 I'd account for every step,
approach God like a prince.
38 If my land cries out against me,
if its furrows weep together,
39 if I gobbled up its produce without paying,
or crushed the life-breath of its tenants,
40 then let thorns grow for wheat,
for barley—weeds!"

Job's words cease.

The Elihu Explosion

As noted in the introduction, the following speeches by Elihu seem like an interruption in the text. Logically it would make more sense to proceed directly from what Job has just said in chapter 31 to the beginning of God's reply to Job in chapter 38. Instead, what we have here is a series of speeches from a character who has not been mentioned before and who is never named or even alluded to after his final speech in chapter 37.

Elihu is introduced here and begins his speech. He opens by explaining that he held his peace until his elders had completed what they had to say. This gesture of respect, however, is quickly undercut by his condemnation of the friends for not refuting Job's arguments. Elihu then goes on to say that he will speak; in fact, he is about to explode with words. His actual argument, however, does not begin until 33:8.

1 "Elihu" means "he is my God"; there is an Elihu in the ancestry of Samuel (1 Samuel 1:1). "Barakel" means "God has blessed"; "the Buzite" refers to the descendants of Buz, a nephew of Abraham (Genesis 22:21). Elihu, unlike the other characters, is given—perhaps ironically—an impeccable Israelite background.

□ Chapter 32

1 And they ceased, the three men, from answering Job, since in his own eyes he was in the right.

2 But Elihu—son of Barakel the Buzite of the Ram clan**1**—burned fiercely with anger against Job in that he had maintained his own rightness rather than God's. 3 And he burned with anger against the three friends, who had not prevailed against Job's arguments and had thereby condemned God. 4 Elihu had waited to speak against Job because they were many years older than he. 5 But when Elihu saw that the three men had run out of things to say, his anger rose up. 6 So Elihu—son of Barakel the Buzite—said:

"I am young in age
and you are elders;
thus I was very much afraid
to tell you what I know.
7 I thought, 'Length of days should speak;
many years teach wisdom.'
8 But one's spirit,
the Mighty One's breath, gives discernment.
9 Wise men are few;
elders may not discern justly.
10 Thus I say: Listen to me!
I too will say what I know.

(continued on page 155)

2 This seems to be a description of the listeners, not a part of Elihu's speech.

11 Look! I waited while you spoke;
I heard your arguments
while you searched for words.
12 I attended fully to you—
but look! Not one of you refuted Job;
nor did any of you answer his statements.

13 "Don't try to say, 'The wisest thing
is to let God, not a human being, refute him.'
14 He hasn't battled me with words,
and I'm not going to answer him with arguments like yours."

15 They are dismayed and answer no further;
words fail them.**2**

16 "Must I wait when they speak no further?
When they stand there with no answers?
17 No! I—yes, I!—will speak my piece!
I—yes, I!—will say what I know!
18 I'm bursting with words,
driven by my inner spirit.
19 Look! Inside I'm wine sealed up,
new wineskins near to bursting.
20 I've got to speak to find relief,
I must open my lips and answer.
21 I'm not biased in anyone's favor;
I flatter no one.
22 If I did know how to flatter,
my Maker would quickly carry me off."

After some beating around the bush, Elihu launches into his speech. His first point is that Job is wrong to think that God does not speak to him or answer him. God appears to us in dreams and night visions to warn us to avoid evil. God also speaks in our pains and sickness, and only the mercy of God, brought about by an angel (or messenger) who takes our part, will rescue us from disease and death. But the absolute necessity for this mercy is that we admit what we have done wrong and ask God for forgiveness and for guidance to avoid sin in the future.

Chapter 33

1 "But now, Job, hear my speech—
attend to my words!
2 Look! I'm opening my mouth,
my tongue and palate form words.
3 What I speak comes from a good heart;
my lips express purely what I know.
4 The spirit of God made me;
the breath of the Mighty One enlivens me.
5 Answer me, if you can;
get ready to face me!
6 Look! Before God our mouths are equal;
I also was pulled from clay!
7 Look! Don't fear me;
my hand won't be heavy on you.

8 "You said—I heard you—
I heard your exact words—
9 'I am pure, having no sin—
I am clean with no guilt.
10 But God finds fault with me,
and treats me as an enemy.
11 God shackles my feet;
God watches every step I take.'

(*continued on page 159*)

1 This assertion is what Eliphaz has already stated in 4:12–15.

12 "But in this you are not right,
since God is greater than human beings.
13 Why do you charge God
with not answering these words?
14 God speaks—one way or another—
though we may not notice.
15 In dreams, night visions—1
when we fall into deep slumber,
sleeping in our beds—
16 God opens our ears,
terrifies us with warnings,
17 to deter us from evil deeds,
to keep us from pride.
18 God saves souls from the grave,
lives from perishing by the sword.

19 "Or one may be disciplined on a bed of pain,
with ever-aching bones,
20 finding food repulsive,
loathing even choice fare.
21 One's flesh wastes,
one's bones, once hidden, stick out,
22 one's soul nears the grave,
one's life nears the death-bringers.
23 Only if an angel stands by one,
a go-between, one in a thousand,
who tells of one's rightness,
24 who is filled with mercy and says,
'Spare him from descending to the grave!
I have come up with the ransom'—
25 then one's flesh is renewed, like a child's,
restored to the days of youth.

(continued on page 161)

2 Elihu's contradictory instructions—"Listen!" "Keep quiet!" "Speak!" "Listen!" "Keep quiet!"—are indicative of his inconsistent arguments in general.

26 "One prays to God—one gains God's favor—
sees God's face joyfully;
God restores one to righteousness.
27 One comes to others and says,
'I sinned—twisted what was right—
but I was not paid with just deserts.
28 God saved my soul from the grave,
and my life sees the light.'
29 Look! All this God does—
twice, three times, for a person—
30 pulling one's soul back from the grave,
into the shining light of life.
31 Attend, Job! Listen to me!**2**
Keep quiet and I'll speak!
32 If you have something to say, say it!
Speak up! I want you made right!
33 If not, listen to me!
Keep quiet and I'll teach you wisdom!"

[⌘] For Elihu, Job's protestations of innocence and righteousness simply make a mockery of God. In truth, Elihu says, God does no wrong; God's punishment is only repayment for human wrongdoing. God punishes all the wicked, whether important or unimportant. No prince or ruler is too powerful, no wealthy person too rich, to escape God's justice. There is no hiding from God. The wicked bring punishment on themselves by oppressing the poor, who then cry to God for justice. Elihu also maintains that someone can repent of sin or injustice and ask for God's guidance, but that is not what Job has done—Job has set himself up as a judge in his own case and thus as more competent than God. He thus reveals himself not merely as a sinner but as a rebel.

☐ Chapter 34

1 Then Elihu said:

2 "Hear me, you wise!

Listen, you learned!

3 The ear tests words

as the tongue tastes food.

4 Let us distinguish what is right;

let us learn among ourselves what is good.

5 Job says, 'I'm righteous,

but God won't treat me justly.

6 Even though I'm just, I must be lying;

I'm not guilty, but his arrow wounds me grievously.'

7 Was there ever anybody like Job?

He guzzles mockery like water,

8 hangs out with evildoers,

consorts with the wicked.

9 He says, 'There's no payoff

in trying to please God.'

10 "Now listen! You who understand;

far be it from God to do ill,

from the Mighty One to do wrong.

11 God repays a person for what that one does,

brings back the consequences upon a person.

12 Truly God does no evil;

the Mighty One never twists justice.

(continued on page 165)

1 This translation assumes that "him" refers to Job, and therefore Elihu's question means, "Who made Job the one in charge of the world?" (Answer: No one.) But it could also refer to God, in which case the question would mean, "What power was great enough to be responsible for putting God in charge of the world?" (Answer: There is no power greater than God, and God was not appointed by anyone.) It is impossible to reflect the ambiguity in this translation.

13 Who set him[1] over the earth?
Who put him in charge of the whole world?
14 If God ever had in mind
to draw back God's spirit and breath,
15 all those living would die together,
and all humankind would return to dust.

16 "If you are discerning, hear this!
Listen to what I have to say!
17 Can anyone who hates justice be a ruler?
Do you condemn the righteous Mighty One?
18 Does one say to a king, 'You're worthless!'—
to nobles, 'You are wicked!'?
19 God shows no partiality to princes,
God does not favor rich over poor,
since they are all God's handiwork.
20 In an instant, at midnight, they die;
people are shaken and pass away;
gone are the mighty by no human act.
21 For God's eyes are upon each person's ways,
each person's steps God sees.
22 No place dark enough, no shadow deep enough
to hide evildoers.
23 God needs no further examination
for anyone who comes before God in judgment.
24 God breaks the mighty with no inquiry,
setting others in their place.
25 Because God notes their acts,
God overthrows them in one night, crushing them.

(continued on page 167)

2   Elihu is asserting that God does indeed hear the needy cry, but if God is silent in response, we have no right to condemn God.

26 For their wickedness God punishes them,
where all can see them,
27 since they turned from God,
disregarding any of God's ways.
28 They caused the cry of the poor to come before God,
so that God heard the needy cry.

29 "But if God is silent, who can condemn?
If God hides God's face, who can see?**2**
Over a nation or over a person, it's all the same:
30 no godless one will rule,
no people be snared.
31 Someone might say to God,
'I'm guilty, but I will offend no more.
32 Guide me! If there's something I don't see,
and I did wrong, I won't do it again.'
33 But you! Shall God reward you on your say-so?
You refuse any decision but your own.
Do you know anything about it? Speak!
34 People of sense say to me—
the wise who hear me say to me—
35 'Job doesn't speak with knowledge,
his words carry no insight.
36 Job should be tested to the limit
for answering like the wicked would!
37 For adding rebellion to his shortcomings,
he claps his hands in scorn at us,
and puts forth even more words against God.'"

⚜ Elihu argues further that it doesn't actually matter whether sin profits someone or not. That is not how God operates, because neither human sin nor human righteousness has any effect on God. This argument is obscure, but the point seems to be that Job's complaint— "If I sinned, what good has it done me?"—is beside the point. If Job has oppressed other human beings, however, that is what has led to his punishment.

1 An obscure statement. It may be paraphrased as follows: "What would you, God, get out of punishing me if I have in fact sinned? And what more could you do to punish me, if I had sinned, than what you've already done?" Elihu is putting Job's argument as "What kind of enjoyment does God get from punishing me for doing nothing wrong? And, if I admit for the moment that I have done something wrong, is there anything more that God could do to me than what God has already done?"

2 In verses 6–7, Elihu turns the argument around and asks, "What effect does Job's sin have upon God?" (Answer: None.) And, "What would God get out of it if Job were righteous?" (Answer: Nothing.)

☐ Chapter 35

1 And Elihu said:

 2 "You think this is justice—
 that you say, 'God will do right by me'?
 3 You ask, 'What do you get from this,
 what do I get from sin?'**1**
 4 I'll answer you,
 and your friends as well.
 5 Look to the heavens! See!
 Regard the clouds high above!
 6 If you have sinned, how does it affect God?
 If your sins are many, how does it affect God?
 7 And if you're righteous, what are you giving God?
 What does God get at your hand?**2**
 8 Your wickedness concerns only others like you,
 your righteousness only other human beings.
 9 They cry out under oppression,
 beg for help against the arms of the great.

(continued on page 171)

3 Elihu here, in contrast to what he says in 34:28, asserts that God pays no heed to the human cry because it arises from arrogance. It is possible that Elihu means to contrast the divine response to the cry of the poor and innocent and the response to Job's complaint, which (in Elihu's view) is an illegitimate plea. But the general confusion surrounding Elihu's argument leaves this unclear, and the impression is that he is arguing on both sides: both that God does hear human laments, and that God "does not hear" (that is, ignores) such pleas.

10 "No one says, 'Where is God who made me—
giving protection in the night,
11 teaching us more than the animals of earth,
making us wiser than birds of the air?'
12 God does not answer**³** when they cry
because of the arrogance of evil.
13 God does not hear the useless plea;
the Mighty One does not attend.
14 So much the less, then, will God listen
if you say you can't see God—
your case is with God—just wait for God—
15 and further, if you say God's anger doesn't punish,
and God doesn't notice wickedness at all.
16 So Job's mouth produces emptiness,
puts forth more words without knowledge."

⟨♪⟩ God cares for the righteous, but if they find themselves afflicted as Job is, it is their responsibility to find out from God what they have done to deserve their suffering. Anyone who, when suffering under punishment, does not cry out for mercy and forgiveness is headed for death. Suffering can lead to repentance, which can bring about restoration of prosperity; but if we persist in evil, even under suffering, we get what we deserve. Above all, Job must remember to praise God and God's works, because God is great in power, as we see through the wonders of creation.

☐ Chapter 36

1 Elihu went on to say:
2 "Just a little longer, while I show you
what more can be said in God's defense.
3 My knowledge comes from afar;
to my Maker I ascribe righteousness.
4 Indeed, my words do not lie;
one perfect in knowledge is with you.

5 "Look! God is majestic
but does not despise any innocent one.
6 God does not keep the wicked alive;
God gives justice to the oppressed.
7 God doesn't take God's eye off the righteous;
God places them on thrones with kings;
they are exalted forever.

8 "But if they are bound in chains,
restrained in the cords of affliction,
9 God tells them what they have done:
they have sinned with insolence.
10 God opens their ears to discipline,
and orders them to turn from evil.
11 If they obey God and serve God,
they will live out their days prosperously,
their years contentedly.
12 If they won't listen, they will perish by sword,
die without knowledge.

(continued on page 175)

1 With repentant sorrow.

2 The text specifies male prostitutes; the reference is to sacred prostitution as a cultic practice. It is very difficult to determine whether this was at all common or even practiced anywhere.

3 Don't commit even more evil in order to escape the affliction that evil has caused you in the first place.

13 "Those who are impious of heart hold anger,
refusing to cry[1] under God's punishment.
14 Their souls are dead at a young age;
their lives end among cult prostitutes.[2]
15 Through suffering God saves sufferers,
through affliction opens their ears.
16 God woos you from the maw of dire straits
into unconfined expanse,
to the comfort of a table laden with choice food.

17 "But now judgment due the wicked weighs you down,
judgment and justice are upon you.
18 Take care! Don't be fooled by riches,
nor diverted by a large bribe.
19 Will your wealth bear you up in dire straits,
all your mighty efforts?
20 Don't long for the night
when people are dragged from their places.
21 Take care! Lest you turn to evil,
favoring it over affliction.[3]

22 "Look! God is supernal in power.
What teacher is like God?
23 Who can tell God how to act?
Who can say to God, 'You're wrong'?
24 Remember: extol God's works,
which human beings have sung praise for.
25 All human beings have seen it;
they regard it from afar.

(continued on page 177)

4 Here begins Elihu's description of the thunderstorm, the natural phenomenon he presents as the best demonstration of God's power and majesty. The description continues, and is expanded, in chapter 37.

26 "Look! God is great, beyond understanding,
age upon age, past comprehending.
27 God draws the water-drops[4]
that condense and rain into the streams,
28 that shower down from the clouds,
pouring abundantly on humankind.
29 Can one understand the clouds spread out,
the thunder from God's dwelling?
30 Look! God scatters God's lights,
reaching the depths of the seas.
31 Thus God rules all peoples,
gives them abundant food.
32 God's hands are filled with lightning,
God aims it at the mark.
33 God's thunder foretells the storm,
even the beasts know it approaches.

⟨✍⟩ Elihu ends his speech in defense of God by extolling the wonders of creation, and specifically the wonders of God's voice in the thunder. Just as we cannot abide the storm or look at the sun, so is God beyond our comprehension. Even to ask to speak to God is to court destruction, to risk being eaten alive. God's power and majesty are far above ours, and God's wisdom is utterly beyond any human understanding.

1 Elihu's limited poetical abilities are perhaps shown most clearly here, in the repetition of the Hebrew word *kol*, "voice": once in verse 2, three times in verse 4, and once in verse 5.

2 When it storms or rains, all human labor ceases, thereby showing God's power.

☐ Chapter 37

1 "Now my heart pounds
and jumps from its place.
2 Listen closely! The roar of God's voice,
the rumble coming from God's mouth,
3 under the whole heaven God looses it,
God's lightning-flashes, to the ends of the earth.
4 After that, God's voice roars,
thundering with majestic voice;
nothing holds back that voice from being heard.
5 God thunders marvelously with God's voice;[1]
God does great things beyond our comprehension.
6 God tells the snow, 'Fall to earth!'
to the rains falling down, 'Rain heavily!'
7 God stops all labor
that all may know God's work.[2]
8 Any living creature takes cover,
staying in its den.
9 The storm bursts from its chamber,
cold from the driving blast.
10 God's breath brings in the ice,
and freezes the wide waters.
11 God stuffs the clouds with moisture,
scatters God's lightning throughout.

(continued on page 181)

179

3 Whether the storm is destructive, nourishing, or comforting, it is God who is in charge of it.

12 "As God wills they change direction;
they do what God commands
throughout the earth.
13 To punish, to feed,
to show mercy, God brings it along.³

14 "Hear this, Job! Stop!
Consider God's wonders!
15 Do you know how God controls this,
making the lightning flash from the clouds?
16 Do you know about the banks of clouds,
the wonders of God's perfect knowledge—
17 you, who sweat in your clothes
when the land lies still under southern heat?
18 Can you, alongside God, spread out the skies
hard as the metal mirror?

19 "Tell us: what do we say to God?
We're in the dark—we can't make our case!
20 Should God be told that I'd want to speak to God?
Does anyone ask to be eaten alive?
21 No one can look at the sun,
bright in the skies
when the wind has cleared them.

22 "From the north comes gold
to God's awesome majesty.
23 We cannot reach the Mighty One;
the height of power and justice,
greatly righteous, God does not oppress.
24 Thus all humankind should stand in awe of God;
God has no regard for even the wisest among us."

The Answer of God from the Storm

Chapters 38–41, in which God speaks directly to Job, are poetical, eloquent, dramatic, and passionate, even though they do not answer Job's questions: Is life really fair? Can God be held accountable for life's sufferings? Is there any justice on earth? Instead, in an outburst that is interrupted only once, God questions Job's very ability to understand the workings of creation, the mysteries of power and order that are necessary for the world to function at all, and the marvels beyond human understanding that are contained within the realm of creation. These marvels are symbolized by God's two greatest examples of creativity, Behemoth and Leviathan. Behemoth seems to be modeled on the hippopotamus, while Leviathan is described in terms that evoke the crocodile of Egypt, a denizen of the Nile River. In both cases, however, the descriptions, although they begin by depicting actual animals, become increasingly mythological and even surreal as they proceed.

Jewish interpretation came up with an interesting view of the ultimate fate of Behemoth and Leviathan. According to the Babylonian Talmud (*Bava Batra* 74b–75a), God prevents both of these creatures from reproducing, lest in their power and ferocity they overwhelm creation. Thus the male is castrated and the female is preserved (in salt or by cooling) until the "last days" when the righteous will sit down at the banquet of God. Behemoth and Leviathan will provide the beef and fish courses, respectively, and will be carved up and served to the faithful, because God will have hooked them, skinned them, and roasted or boiled them (all of which is derived from the various poetical descriptions of the creatures in water, breathing fire, making the seas steam like a cauldron, and so on). This interpretation in particular seems to have been inspired by the near-mythical language used of the creatures, particularly of Leviathan.

At the start of chapter 38, God begins immediately not to answer Job but to barrage him with questions. They show that because Job has no power over the universe and no responsibility for controlling or governing it, he has no right to query the justice of the created order. God's questions take in the whole range of creation, from light and darkness to rain, snow, and ice, wind and stars, lions and ravens, and finally to the sources of human wisdom and discernment.

1 The image of God controlling the sea in verses 8–11 evokes the mythological motif of creation as a battle in which chaos is overcome and conquered.

☐ Chapter 38

1 Then the L ORD answered Job
from amid the storm and said:
    2 "Who is this dimming counsel
    with words but no knowledge?
    3 Gird up your loins like a man!
    I'll ask questions, and you will answer!
    4 Where were you when I formed Earth?
    Tell me—you understand things!
    5 Who set out its limits? You must know!
    Who laid out its measurements?
    6 What is it based on?
    Who laid its cornerstone—
    7 while all the morning stars sang in chorus
    and the heavenly beings shouted out for joy?
    8 Who shut the Sea behind doors
    when it would rush from the womb—
    9 when I clothed it with clouds,
    swathed it in darkness,
    10 when I set its limits,
    fixed the bars and doors,
    11 said, 'Thus far you may come, but no farther;
    here your haughty waves halt'?[1]

    12 "Have you ever arranged for the morning,
    put the dawn in place,

(continued on page 187)

2 The image is of the morning or the dawn grabbing darkness, as one would take hold of a skirt or robe, and pulling it off the earth as a robe is taken off and shaken out. The imagery may in fact convey the rapid disrobing of a woman and could be translated "strip Earth's cloak of darkness from her." The shaking out of the garment is meant to compare the wicked (who carry out their schemes under cover of darkness) to fleas or lice being shaken off an article of clothing.

3 The shapes of things appear slowly as dawn approaches and finally breaks, and what has seemed formless in the dark becomes like the impress of a seal on a lump of clay or like the dye patterns appearing on cloth.

4 The mention of light coming with the dawn leads to the image of the wicked who regard darkness as light, because they do their work under cover of night. The plans of the wicked are foiled in the day when their "light" (meaning darkness) is taken from them; the arm they have raised, presumably to commit murder or robbery, is thus broken. See 24:13–17.

13 to take the cloak of darkness from Earth
and shake the wicked out of it?[2]
14 The earth shows its shapes, like clay from a seal,
like patterns on a garment.[3]
15 The light of the wicked is taken from them,
their upraised arm is broken.[4]

16 "Have you traveled where the sea wells up,
or walked in the clefts of the deep?
17 Were the gates of death revealed to you?
Have you seen the gloomy gates?
18 Have you grasped earth's huge expanse?
Speak up if you know all this!

19 "Which way to the dwelling of light?
Where is dark's abode?
20 Can you show each to its place?
Do you truly know its way home?
21 Of course you know! You were born before they were!
The days of your life are great in number.

22 "Have you gone into the snow stockpiles,
or seen the stockpiles of hail?
23 Those I save up for troubled times,
for war and battle-days.
24 What route scatters the lightning
or spreads the east wind around the earth?
25 Who cuts channels for the pouring rain,
makes paths for the thunderstorm,
26 watering the uninhabited land,
the empty wilderness,
27 to feed the barren waste,
greening it with grass?

(continued on page 189)

It is unclear whether the lumps and clumps are dried soil that dissolves in rain or mud clods that are created when the rain falls.

28 Does rain have a father?
Who sires the dewdrops?
29 Whose womb bears the ice?
Who births the frosts of heaven—
30 as the waters harden like stone
and the face of the deep freezes?

31 "Can you fasten fetters on the Pleiades?
Can you loose the cords of Orion?
32 Can you bring out each constellation in its season,
leading the Great Bear and its little ones?
33 Do you know the heavenly ordinances,
or can you arrange the rulings for the earth?

34 "Can your voice reach the clouds?
Can you cover yourself with floods?
35 Do you send off the lightning bolts?
Do they say to you, 'Here we are!'
36 Who puts wisdom deep within a person,
or who gives discernment to the thinker?
37 Who has the wisdom to count the clouds,
who can upend the heaven's water-jars
38 when the dust forms lumps
and the clods of soil clump?[5]

39 "Do you hunt prey for the lioness,
feed the hungry lions,
40 as they crouch in a den,
lie in wait in the bushes?
41 Who furnishes food for the raven,
when its chicks cry to God,
searching aimlessly for feed?"

⟨𝒶⟩ God's questions continue on from the end of the previous chapter, raising matters having to do with the lives of animals: they produce and rear their young, who in turn flourish and run free, all without any human direction. Even a domesticated animal like the horse still acts in accordance with its wild nature when it is ridden into battle. The animals include the goat, the donkey, the ox, the ostrich, the horse, the hawk, and the eagle.

1 The donkey or wild ass does not subject itself to urban life and never submits to being driven by anyone, so never hears the shouts of someone trying to direct it.

2 In harrowing, which involves dragging a spiked implement through a field in order to clear it of roots from the previous crop, the laborer leads while the draught animal follows, the reverse of the arrangement for plowing.

☐ Chapter 39

1 "Do you know when the wild goats give birth,
or oversee the doe bearing her fawn,
2 counting the months of their full term,
knowing their birth-time has come?
3 They crouch, their labor brings forth young,
birthing the little being in the open.
4 The little ones thrive and grow in the wild;
they leave and don't come back.

5 "Who set the wild donkey free?
Who untied the wild ass's tethers?
6 I gave him wilderness for a home,
salt flats for a dwelling.
7 He derides the noise of towns,
nor does he hear the drover's shout.[1]
8 He roves the hillside for pasture,
seeking anything green.

9 "Will the wild ox agree to serve you?
Will he remain by night at your trough?
10 Can you keep him to the furrow with harness?
Will he follow you with the harrow through the valley?[2]
11 Do you count on his great strength?
Do you leave the heavy work to him?
12 Can you trust him to come back,
bringing the grain to your threshing floor?

(continued on page 193)

3 The ostrich was proverbially a neglectful parent.

4 A running ostrich was thought to be faster than horse and rider. The ostrich can in fact run at speeds over forty miles an hour, while a running horse usually averages thirty miles an hour, although it can go faster for short bursts. In general, however, an ostrich can outrun a horse.

5 Or, "the trumpet sounds—he cannot hold still!"

13 "The ostrich's wings flap noisily—
no stork-like feathers for her.
14 She lays her eggs on the ground,
warms them in the sand,
15 careless that any foot might crush them,
and wild beast might trample them.
16 She is hard on her offspring,
not caring that her labor might be in vain,
17 for God gave her no wisdom,
provided her no discernment.[3]
18 Yet when she spreads out her plumes
she laughs back at horse and rider.[4]

19 "Do you provide strength to the horse?
Drape his neck with a flowing mane?
20 Do you have him leap like the locust,
his prideful snort bringing terror?
21 He paws violently, joying in strength,
charging into the fight.
22 He laughs at fear, not abashed at anything,
not even shying from the sword's edge.
23 The quiver rattles at his side,
spear and lance flash,
24 he dashes across the ground in excited frenzy,
nor pauses for the trumpet sound.[5]
25 Whenever it trumpets, he snorts, Aha!
He scents battle far off,
the officers' shouts, the battle cry.

(continued on page 195)

6 Partly by association of ideas, the poet has God present the birds of prey—hawk and eagle—and then circles back to the battlefield that the horse has scented just before.

26 "Is it by your wisdom the hawk**6** soars,
spreading his wings southwards?
27 Does the eagle mount up when you command,
building his lofty aerie?
28 On a cliff he dwells, remaining at night;
his stronghold is a rock crag.
29 From there he spies the prey;
his eyes can spot it from afar.
30 His young brood feast on blood;
he is there where the slain are."

After a brief exchange with Job, God resumes the questions with a series that challenges Job's power (and therefore Job's right to question God's justice), particularly Job's power to overthrow the mighty and proud or the wicked. God then turns, by association of ideas, to Behemoth and his strength. Behemoth seems to be modeled on the hippopotamus, though the descriptions of his prodigious appetite (verse 20) and his ability to withstand floods (verse 23) ascribe more than natural size and strength to him. Just as Job cannot control the proud and wicked, so Job, God implies, cannot control Behemoth.

1 A metaphor for strength or power.

☐ Chapter 40

1 The LORD said to Job:
2 "The one who contends with the Mighty One—does he yield?
The one accusing God—let him answer!"

3 Then Job answered the LORD:
4 "Look! I am not worthy to reply to you;
I lay my hand over my mouth.
5 I spoke once—I won't reply;
twice, but will say no more."

6 Then the LORD answered Job from amid the storm, and said:
7 "Gird your loins like a man!
I'll ask you—you answer me!
8 Would you indeed devalue my justice—
condemn me to make yourself righteous?
9 You have an arm[1] like God?
Your voice can thunder like God's?
10 Bedeck yourself, then, with grandeur, splendor,
array yourself with majesty and glory.
11 Loose your wrathful fury!
Look at the proud and bring them low!
12 Look at the proud! Humble them!
Crush the wicked where they are!
13 Bury them together in the dust;
cover their faces in the grave.
14 Then indeed I will acknowledge to you
that your own right hand can save you.

(continued on page 199)

198 The Book of Job

| 2 | Behemoth is a Hebrew plural form for the feminine noun *behemah*, which means "beast" or "animal," usually used more narrowly to mean "livestock" or "cattle," as in Genesis 1:24. In Joel 1:20 the plural form means "[wild] animals." Here, though the form is plural, it is the plural used to denote greatness or majesty; all the verbs are masculine singular, and therefore Behemoth is translated using the pronoun "he."

| 3 | The tail and thighs could be euphemisms for the phallus and testicles. Part of the strength of the beast is therefore his potency and generativity.

| 4 | The appetite of Behemoth is so great that he eats not only aquatic plants but also the growth on hillsides. But he does not eat flesh, so other animals are safe from him.

| 5 | The beast floats in the water, so he is safe even when the water rises (in a storm or from spring runoff). The only parts of him that are visible are his eyes and nose, thus leading to the question of whether anyone would try to capture him by the eyes or by a hook through the nose.

15 "Look! Here is Behemoth[2]
that I made as I made you.
16 Look at the strength in his loins,
the muscle power of his belly.
17 His tail stands like a cedar;
his thigh sinews are tight-knit.[3]
18 His bones are bronze pipes,
his limbs iron bars.
19 He is first among God's works,
and only his Maker can overpower him.
20 He eats up even the hill growth,
but wild animals frolic safely nearby.[4]
21 Under the lotus he lies,
concealed among marsh reeds.
22 The lotus hides him in shadow,
the marsh trees surround him.
23 The river may rage, but he doesn't fear;
he is safe though the whole of Jordan rise to his mouth.
24 Who would dare grab him by his eyes
or hook him through the nose?"[5]

⟨⟩ In the last of God's speeches, the subject is Leviathan, apparently modeled on the crocodile—thick and scaly hide, rows of teeth, aggressive and ferocious behavior. As with the description of Behemoth, though even more so, the attributes of Leviathan become more and more mythical as the chapter goes on, until he is being described as breathing fire and lightning (verses 18–21), making the sea boil (verse 31), and having virtually impenetrable skin, like a suit of armor (verses 15–17, 26–30).

1 Leviathan means "coiled" or "twisted," and some of the descriptive text, as noted above, seems to evoke the crocodile. Elsewhere in the Bible (Isaiah 27:1; Psalm 104:26) Leviathan is a sea serpent or perhaps a whale.

2 This beast is seen as unparalleled in ferocity.

3 This verse interrupts the description and may have been inserted later. It means that there is no one who can charge God with not meeting obligations, especially because God owns everything and can be obliged to no one.

☐ Chapter 41

1 "Can you pull in Leviathan[1] with a hook,
tie down his tongue with rope?
2 Can you thread cord through his nose—
hook him by his jaw?
3 You think he'll beg for mercy?
Speak tenderly to you?
4 Will he seal a pact with you,
will you have him as a slave-for-life?
5 Can you make him your pet, like a bird,
or leash him for your little girls?
6 Will traders haggle over him,
or meat sellers divvy him up?
7 Will you stick his hide full of harpoons,
or his head full of fishing spears?

8 "Go ahead! Try to put your hand on him!
He'll give you a battle you won't forget!
9 Subduing him is but a false hope;
simply to see him is to be overcome.
10 None so fierce as to rouse him—
who can stand against him?"[2]

11 ["Is there any to put in a claim against me for payment?
Everything under heaven is mine!"][3]

(continued on page 203)

4 The crocodile's ribbed and scaly hide is depicted in verses 15–17 as a garment of armor, which would have consisted of metal disks sewn onto a cloth and worn in order to turn aside arrows.

5 The clearly mythological description resembles later depictions of fire-breathing dragons.

12 "I will not be silent about his limbs,
nor omit his strength, his graceful form.
13 Who can remove his outer coat?
Who can come near him with a bridle?
14 Who can open the doors of his mouth—
ranged as they are with terrible teeth?
15 His back is rows of shields,
sealed tightly closed—
16 each so close to the next
no breath can pass between—
17 one joined to the other,
they stick fast, inseparable.[4]

18 "His sneezes are lightning flashes,
his eyes are rays of dawn.
19 Flames stream from his mouth,
shooting-sparks of fire.
20 Smoke pours from his nostrils
like a boiling pot on blazing reeds.
21 His breath like glowing coal,
flame blazing from his mouth.[5]

22 "Strength lives in his neck;
despair precedes him.
23 His flesh folded tightly
does not move in its firmness.
24 His chest is rock-solid,
like the lower millstone.
25 When he rears up, even the mighty are terrified;
they draw back from his thrashing.

(continued on page 205)

6 Leviathan is superior to every other created being, so God, in being able to create and control Leviathan, is therefore shown to be more powerful than all of creation combined.

26 "No sword affects him—
nor spear, dart, or javelin.
27 Iron is like straw to him,
bronze like rotten wood.
28 No arrow puts him to flight,
and slingstones hit him like chaff.
29 Clubs are like splinters;
he laughs at lances.
30 His undersides are as if caked with shards,
and he drags through mud like a thresher.

31 "He makes the sea a churning cauldron,
like a pot of boiling ointment.
32 Behind him the wake gleams,
as if the sea had white hair.

33 "There's not his equal on earth,
one formed to be fearless.
34 He looks down on all that is lofty,[6]
king over all the children of pride."

Job's Final Reply

The end of the book of Job is in two parts: a six-verse, poetical apology from Job, quoting God and expressing humility and repentance; and an eleven-verse, prose conclusion that quickly undoes all the calamities from the opening story and gives God's final assessment of the arguments of the friends.

Job quotes from God's opening speech, 38:2,3.

□ Chapter 42

1 Then Job answered the LORD:
2 "I know you can do anything;
no plan of yours can be foiled.
3 'Who is this dimming counsel without knowledge?'
I spoke without understanding
of marvels beyond my grasp.
4 'Listen, I will speak!
I'll ask questions, and you will answer!'**1**
5 By hearing only had I heard of you
but now my eye sees you.
6 So I abase myself for it
and repent in dust and ashes."

The Prose Framework: Closing

The restoration of Job's fortunes and family in this closing section brings the frame story full circle. This folk tale is not meant to be realistic: the size of Job's various herds, the length of his life, and most of all, the "replacement" family he is granted, are all motifs of storytelling that are characteristic of this literary form.

1 "Dove" in Hebrew is Jemimah; "Cinnamon" is Keziah; "Dark Eyes" is a loose rendition of Keren-happuch, "horn of eye shadow" or "horn of kohl."

2 Daughters did not usually inherit alongside sons, because they were expected to marry and live with their husbands' families.

☐ Chapter 42
(VERSES 7-17)

7 When the LORD had said these things to Job, the LORD said to Eliphaz the Temanite, "My anger blazes against you and your two friends because you have not spoken rightly about me, as my servant Job has. 8 So, take for yourselves seven bulls and seven rams, go to my servant Job, and sacrifice for yourselves a burnt offering; and my servant Job will pray for you; I will countenance his prayer and not treat you according to your folly; because you have not spoken rightly about me, as my servant Job has." 9 So Eliphaz the Temanite, Bildad the Shuhite, and Zophar the Naamathite did as the LORD commanded; and the LORD countenanced them for Job's sake.

10 The LORD then restored Job's fortunes, after he had prayed for his friends, and the LORD made it twice as much. 11 All his brothers and all his sisters and all his former acquaintances came and consoled him for all the trouble the LORD had brought on him. And they each gave him a silver coin and a gold ring. 12 And the LORD blessed Job's latter days more than the former; he now had fourteen thousand sheep, six thousand camels, a thousand yoke of oxen, and a thousand donkeys. 13 He had seven sons and three daughters. 14 He named the first daughter Dove; the second's name was Cinnamon; the third's name was Dark Eyes.[1] 15 Nowhere else in all the land were women to be found as beautiful as Job's daughters. Their father gave them inheritance rights along with their brothers.[2] 16 Afterwards Job lived 140 years; he saw his children and children's children to four generations. 17 Thus Job died, old, having had a full life.

Acknowledgments ☐

Any effort to "explain" a work as difficult and profound as the book of Job is bound to fall short. My debts to the many scholars who have written on this text are partially represented in the listing of sources and recommendations for further reading at the end of the book.

But I also owe a debt of gratitude to a number of willing conversation partners, particularly those members and friends at my local parish, St. Giles' Episcopal Church in Jefferson, Maine, who met with me on a weekly basis and let me try out some of the ideas contained in the introduction and comments here. They included John Atwood, the Reverend Deacon Lee Burns, George Van Deventer, Colby Dill, Jean Greenwood, David Greer, Susan Greer, D. "Buzz" Marden, Ken Marden, Jean Miller, Cynthia White, and my wife, the Reverend Dr. Susan Kraus, Rector of St. Giles'.

Susan and I have also had a long-running conversation—one that has now gone on for four decades and counting—on the meaning of evil, suffering, and the love of God. We have not succeeded, any more than Job has, in resolving this group of related problems, but we have certainly covered a lot of territory, and there are many ideas in this book that have arisen from that conversation. I thank her profoundly.

My multitalented editors, Cynthia Shattuck, Justine Earnest, and Emily Wichland, all worked to improve my explanations and simplify my some-times convoluted language. Emily's comments shaped the entire project early on and gave it strength and direction. Justine edited the whole book with care and sensitivity. Cynthia has worked over the entire text, and her sure eye for clarity and directness has made it much more readable, and much more approachable, than it would have been otherwise.

Notwithstanding all this help, there are, I am sure, errors of fact and judgment in this book, and those errors are my responsibility alone. But this is a much better book for all the efforts of those who were willing to work through these ideas with me, and I thank you all.

Suggestions for Further Reading ☐

For most general readers, the best way to begin the study of Job is not with a full-fledged commentary but rather with a good study Bible, to grasp the main issues. Three recommendations are included here. Another good place to start is Robert Alter's translation of *The Wisdom Books*, a sensitive and poetical rendering accompanied with careful notes about ambiguities and literary characteristics of the text. Various introductions can also provide general background in biblical literature. The list of books commenting on, discussing, and translating Job is immense; the list here is only intended to give readers a place to start.

Alter, Robert. *The Wisdom Books: Job, Proverbs, and Ecclesiastes: A Translation with Commentary.* New York: W. W. Norton and Company, 2010.

Attridge, Harold W., Wayne A. Meeks, Jouette M. Bassler, Werner E. Lemke, Susan Niditch, and Eileen M. Schuller, eds. *The HarperCollins Study Bible: New Revised Standard Version Including the Apocryphal/Deuterocanonical Books.* Rev. ed. San Francisco: HarperCollins Publishers, 2006.

Berlin, Adele, and Marc Zvi Brettler. *The Jewish Study Bible.* New York: Oxford University Press, 2004.

Coogan, Michael D., Marc Z. Brettler, Carol A. Newsom, and Pheme Perkins, eds. *The New Oxford Annotated Bible: New Revised Standard Version with the Apocrypha.* 4th ed. New York: Oxford University Press, 2010.

Crenshaw, James L. *Defending God: Biblical Responses to the Problem of Evil.* New York: Oxford University Press, 2005.

Davis, Ellen F. *Getting Involved with God: Rediscovering the Old Testament.* Cambridge, MA: Cowley Publications, 2001.

———. *Proverbs, Ecclesiastes, and the Song of Songs.* Louisville, KY: Westminster John Knox Press, 2000.

Glatzer, Nahum N., ed. *The Dimensions of Job: A Study and Selected Readings.* New York: Schocken Books, 1969.

Janzen, J. Gerald. *Job: Interpretation: A Bible Commentary for Teaching and Preaching.* Atlanta: John Knox Press, 1985.

Murphy, Roland E. *The Tree of Life: An Exploration of Biblical Wisdom Literature.* 3rd ed. Grand Rapids, MI: Wm. B. Eerdmans Publishing Company, 2002.

Newsom, Carol A. *The Book of Job: A Contest of Moral Imaginations.* New York: Oxford University Press, 2003.

Pope, Marvin H., ed. *Job: A New Translation with Introduction and Commentary.* 3rd ed. The Anchor Bible 15. Garden City, NY: Doubleday, 1973.

Shapiro, Rami, trans. and ann. *Ecclesiastes: Annotated and Explained.* Woodstock, VT: SkyLight Paths Publishing, 2010.

———. *Proverbs: Annotated and Explained.* Woodstock, VT: SkyLight Paths Publishing, 2011.

von Rad, Gerhard. *Wisdom in Israel.* Translated by James D. Martin. Nashville: Abingdon Press, 1972.

Spirituality & Crafts

Beading—The Creative Spirit: Finding Your Sacred Center through the Art of Beadwork by Rev. Wendy Ellsworth
Invites you on a spiritual pilgrimage into the kaleidoscope world of glass and color. 7 x 9, 240 pp, 8-page color insert, 40+ b/w photos and 40 diagrams, Quality PB, 978-1-59473-267-6 **$18.99**

Contemplative Crochet: A Hands-On Guide for Interlocking Faith and Craft by Cindy Crandall-Frazier; Foreword by Linda Skolnik
Illuminates the spiritual lessons you can learn through crocheting.
7 x 9, 208 pp, b/w photos, Quality PB, 978-1-59473-238-6 **$16.99**

The Knitting Way: A Guide to Spiritual Self-Discovery
by Linda Skolnik and Janice MacDaniels Examines how you can explore and strengthen your spiritual life through knitting.
7 x 9, 240 pp, b/w photos, Quality PB, 978-1-59473-079-5 **$16.99**

The Painting Path: Embodying Spiritual Discovery through Yoga, Brush and Color by Linda Novick; Foreword by Richard Segalman
Explores the divine connection you can experience through art.
7 x 9, 208 pp, 8-page color insert, plus b/w photos, Quality PB, 978-1-59473-226-3 **$18.99**

The Quilting Path: A Guide to Spiritual Discovery through Fabric, Thread and Kabbalah by Louise Silk
Explores how to cultivate personal growth through quilt making.
7 x 9, 192 pp, b/w photos and illus., Quality PB, 978-1-59473-206-5 **$16.99**

The Scrapbooking Journey: A Hands-On Guide to Spiritual Discovery
by Cory Richardson-Lauve; Foreword by Stacy Julian Reveals how this craft can become a practice used to deepen and shape your life.
7 x 9, 176 pp, 8-page color insert, plus b/w photos, Quality PB, 978-1-59473-216-4 **$18.99**

The Soulwork of Clay: A Hands-On Approach to Spirituality
by Marjory Zoet Bankson; Photos by Peter Bankson
Takes you through the seven-step process of making clay into a pot, drawing parallels at each stage to the process of spiritual growth.
7 x 9, 192 pp, b/w photos, Quality PB, 978-1-59473-249-2 **$16.99**

Kabbalah / Enneagram
(Books from Jewish Lights Publishing, SkyLight Paths' sister imprint)

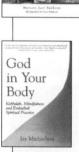

Cast in God's Image: Discover Your Personality Type Using the Enneagram and Kabbalah
by Rabbi Howard A. Addison, PhD 7 x 9, 176 pp, Quality PB, 978-1-58023-124-4 **$16.95**

Ehyeh: A Kabbalah for Tomorrow by Rabbi Arthur Green, PhD
6 x 9, 224 pp, Quality PB, 978-1-58023-213-5 **$18.99**

The Enneagram and Kabbalah, 2nd Edition: Reading Your Soul
by Rabbi Howard A. Addison, PhD 6 x 9, 192 pp, Quality PB, 978-1-58023-229-6 **$16.99**

The Gift of Kabbalah: Discovering the Secrets of Heaven, Renewing Your Life on Earth
by Tamar Frankiel, PhD 6 x 9, 256 pp, Quality PB, 978-1-58023-141-1 **$16.95**

God in Your Body: Kabbalah, Mindfulness and Embodied Spiritual Practice
by Jay Michaelson 6 x 9, 272 pp, Quality PB, 978-1-58023-304-0 **$18.99**

Jewish Mysticism and the Spiritual Life: Classical Texts, Contemporary Reflections
Edited by Dr. Lawrence Fine, Dr. Eitan Fishbane and Rabbi Or N. Rose
6 x 9, 256 pp, HC, 978-1-58023-434-4 **$24.99**

Kabbalah: A Brief Introduction for Christians
by Tamar Frankiel, PhD 5½ x 8½, 208 pp, Quality PB, 978-1-58023-303-3 **$16.99**

Zohar: Annotated & Explained Translation & Annotation by Daniel C. Matt;
Foreword by Andrew Harvey 5½ x 8½, 176 pp, Quality PB, 978-1-893361-51-5 **$15.99**

Women's Interest

Women, Spirituality and Transformative Leadership
Where Grace Meets Power
Edited by Kathe Schaaf, Kay Lindahl, Kathleen S. Hurty, PhD, and Reverend Guo Cheen
A dynamic conversation on the power of women's spiritual leadership and its emerging patterns of transformation.
6 x 9, 288 pp, Hardcover, 978-1-59473-313-0 **$24.99**

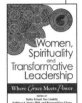

Spiritually Healthy Divorce: Navigating Disruption with Insight & Hope
by Carolyne Call A spiritual map to help you move through the twists and turns of divorce. 6 x 9, 224 pp, Quality PB, 978-1-59473-288-1 **$16.99**

New Feminist Christianity: Many Voices, Many Views
Edited by Mary E. Hunt and Diann L. Neu
Insights from ministers and theologians, activists and leaders, artists and liturgists who are shaping the future. Taken together, their voices offer a starting point for building new models of religious life and worship.
6 x 9, 384 pp, HC, 978-1-59473-285-0 **$24.99**

New Jewish Feminism: Probing the Past, Forging the Future
Edited by Rabbi Elyse Goldstein; Foreword by Anita Diamant
Looks at the growth and accomplishments of Jewish feminism and what they mean for Jewish women today and tomorrow. Features the voices of women from every area of Jewish life, addressing the important issues that concern Jewish women.
6 x 9, 480 pp, Quality PB, 978-1-58023-448-1 **$19.99**; HC, 978-1-58023-359-0 **$24.99***

Bread, Body, Spirit: Finding the Sacred in Food
Edited and with Introductions by Alice Peck 6 x 9, 224 pp, Quality PB, 978-1-59473-242-3 **$19.99**

Dance—The Sacred Art: The Joy of Movement as a Spiritual Practice
by Cynthia Winton-Henry 5½ x 8½, 224 pp, Quality PB, 978-1-59473-268-3 **$16.99**

Daughters of the Desert: Stories of Remarkable Women from Christian, Jewish and Muslim Traditions
by Claire Rudolf Murphy, Meghan Nuttall Sayres, Mary Cronk Farrell, Sarah Conover and Betsy Wharton
5½ x 8½, 192 pp, Illus., Quality PB, 978-1-59473-106-8 **$14.99** Inc. reader's discussion guide

The Divine Feminine in Biblical Wisdom Literature
Selections Annotated & Explained
Translation & Annotation by Rabbi Rami Shapiro; Foreword by Rev. Cynthia Bourgeault, PhD
5½ x 8½, 240 pp, Quality PB, 978-1-59473-109-9 **$16.99**

Divining the Body: Reclaim the Holiness of Your Physical Self
by Jan Phillips 8 x 8, 256 pp, Quality PB, 978-1-59473-080-1 **$16.99**

Honoring Motherhood: Prayers, Ceremonies & Blessings
Edited and with Introductions by Lynn L. Caruso 5 x 7¼, 272 pp, HC, 978-1-59473-239-3 **$19.99**

Next to Godliness: Finding the Sacred in Housekeeping
Edited by Alice Peck 6 x 9, 224 pp, Quality PB, 978-1-59473-214-0 **$19.99**

ReVisions: Seeing Torah through a Feminist Lens
by Rabbi Elyse Goldstein 5½ x 8½, 224 pp, Quality PB, 978-1-58023-117-6 **$16.95***

The Triumph of Eve & Other Subversive Bible Tales
by Matt Biers-Ariel 5½ x 8½, 192 pp, Quality PB, 978-1-59473-176-1 **$14.99**

White Fire: A Portrait of Women Spiritual Leaders in America
by Malka Drucker; Photos by Gay Block 7 x 10, 320 pp, b/w photos, HC, 978-1-893361-64-5 **$24.95**

Woman Spirit Awakening in Nature: Growing Into the Fullness of Who You Are
by Nancy Barrett Chickerneo, PhD; Foreword by Eileen Fisher
8 x 8, 224 pp, b/w illus., Quality PB, 978-1-59473-250-8 **$16.99**

Women of Color Pray: Voices of Strength, Faith, Healing, Hope and Courage
Edited and with Introductions by Christal M. Jackson
5 x 7¼, 208 pp, Quality PB, 978-1-59473-077-1 **$15.99**

The Women's Torah Commentary: New Insights from Women Rabbis on the 54 Weekly Torah Portions *Edited by Rabbi Elyse Goldstein*
6 x 9, 496 pp, Quality PB, 978-1-58023-370-5 **$19.99**; HC, 978-1-58023-076-6 **$34.95***

* A book from Jewish Lights, SkyLight Paths' sister imprint

Sacred Texts
JUDAISM

The Book of Job: Annotated & Explained
Translation & Annotation by Donald Kraus; Foreword by Dr. Marc Brettler
Clarifies for today's readers what Job is, how to overcome difficulties in the text, and suggests what it may mean for us.
5½ x 8½, 256 pp, Quality PB, 978-1-59473-389-5 **$16.99**

The Divine Feminine in Biblical Wisdom Literature
Selections Annotated & Explained
Translation & Annotation by Rabbi Rami Shapiro; Foreword by Rev. Cynthia Bourgeault, PhD
Uses the Hebrew Bible and Wisdom literature to explain Sophia's way of wisdom and illustrate Her creative energy.
5½ x 8½, 240 pp, Quality PB, 978-1-59473-109-9 **$16.99**

Ecclesiastes: Annotated & Explained
Translation & Annotation by Rabbi Rami Shapiro; Foreword by Rev. Barbara Cawthorne Crafton
A timeless teaching on living well amid uncertainty and insecurity.
5½ x 8½, 160 pp, Quality PB, 978-1-59473-287-4 **$16.99**

Ethics of the Sages: *Pirke Avot*—Annotated & Explained
Translation & Annotation by Rabbi Rami Shapiro
Clarifies the ethical teachings of the early Rabbis.
5½ x 8½, 192 pp, Quality PB, 978-1-59473-207-2 **$16.99**

Hasidic Tales: Annotated & Explained
Translation & Annotation by Rabbi Rami Shapiro; Foreword by Andrew Harvey
Introduces the legendary tales of the impassioned Hasidic rabbis, presenting them as stories rather than as parables.
5½ x 8½, 240 pp, Quality PB, 978-1-893361-86-7 **$16.95**

The Hebrew Prophets: Selections Annotated & Explained
Translation & Annotation by Rabbi Rami Shapiro;
Foreword by Rabbi Zalman M. Schachter-Shalomi
5½ x 8½, 224 pp, Quality PB, 978-1-59473-037-5 **$16.99**

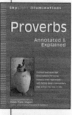

Maimonides—Essential Teachings on Jewish Faith & Ethics
The Book of Knowledge & the Thirteen Principles of Faith—Annotated & Explained
Translation and Annotation by Rabbi Marc D. Angel, PhD
Opens up for us Maimonides's views on the nature of God, providence, prophecy, free will, human nature, repentance and more.
5½ x 8½, 224 pp, Quality PB, 978-1-59473-311-6 **$18.99**

Proverbs: Annotated & Explained
Translation and Annotation by Rabbi Rami Shapiro
Demonstrates how these complex poetic forms are actually straightforward instructions to live simply, without rationalizations and excuses.
5½ x 8½, 288 pp, Quality PB, 978-1-59473-310-9 $16.99

Tanya, the Masterpiece of Hasidic Wisdom
Selections Annotated & Explained
Translation & Annotation by Rabbi Rami Shapiro; Foreword by Rabbi Zalman M. Schachter-Shalomi
Clarifies one of the most powerful and potentially transformative books of Jewish wisdom.
5½ x 8½, 240 pp, Quality PB, 978-1-59473-275-1 **$16.99**

Zohar: Annotated & Explained
Translation & Annotation by Daniel C. Matt; Foreword by Andrew Harvey
The canonical text of Jewish mystical tradition.
5½ x 8½, 176 pp, Quality PB, 978-1-893361-51-5 **$16.99**

Judaism / Christianity / Islam / Interfaith

All Politics Is Religious: Speaking Faith to the Media, Policy Makers and Community   *By Rabbi Dennis S. Ross; Foreword by Rev. Barry W. Lynn*
Provides ideas and strategies for expressing a clear, forceful and progressive religious point of view that is all too often overlooked and under-represented in public discourse.   6 x 9, 192 pp, Quality PB, 978-1-59473-374-1 **$18.99**

Religion Gone Astray: What We Found at the Heart of Interfaith
By Pastor Don Mackenzie, Rabbi Ted Falcon and Imam Jamal Rahman
Welcome to the deeper dimensions of interfaith dialogue—exploring that which divides us personally, spiritually and institutionally.
6 x 9, 192 pp, Quality PB, 978-1-59473-317-8 **$16.99**

Getting to the Heart of Interfaith: The Eye-Opening, Hope-Filled Friendship of a Pastor, a Rabbi & an Imam   *by Pastor Don Mackenzie, Rabbi Ted Falcon and Imam Jamal Rahman*
6 x 9, 192 pp, Quality PB, 978-1-59473-263-8 **$16.99**

Hearing the Call across Traditions: Readings on Faith and Service
Edited by Adam Davis; Foreword by Eboo Patel
6 x 9, 352 pp, Quality PB, 978-1-59473-303-1 **$18.99**; HC, 978-1-59473-264-5 **$29.99**

How to Do Good & Avoid Evil: A Global Ethic from the Sources of Judaism
by Hans Küng and Rabbi Walter Homolka; Translated by Rev. Dr. John Bowden
6 x 9, 224 pp, HC, 978-1-59473-255-3 **$19.99**

Blessed Relief: What Christians Can Learn from Buddhists about Suffering
by Gordon Peerman   6 x 9, 208 pp, Quality PB, 978-1-59473-252-2 **$16.99**

Christians & Jews—Faith to Faith: Tragic History, Promising Present, Fragile Future   *by Rabbi James Rudin*   6 x 9, 288 pp, HC, 978-1-58023-432-0 **$24.99***

Christians & Jews in Dialogue: Learning in the Presence of the Other   *by Mary C. Boys and Sara S. Lee; Foreword by Dorothy C. Bass*   6 x 9, 240 pp, Quality PB, 978-1-59473-254-6 **$18.99**

InterActive Faith: The Essential Interreligious Community-Building Handbook
Edited by Rev. Bud Heckman with Rori Picker Neiss; Foreword by Rev. Dirk Ficca
6 x 9, 304 pp, Quality PB, 978-1-59473-273-7 **$16.99**; HC, 978-1-59473-237-9 **$29.99**

The Jewish Approach to God: A Brief Introduction for Christians
by Rabbi Neil Gillman, PhD   5½ x 8½, 192 pp, Quality PB, 978-1-58023-190-9 **$16.95***

The Jewish Approach to Repairing the World (*Tikkun Olam*): A Brief Introduction for Christians   *by Rabbi Elliot N. Dorff, PhD, with Rev. Cory Willson*
5½ x 8½, 256 pp, Quality PB, 978-1-58023-349-1 **$16.99***

The Jewish Connection to Israel, the Promised Land: A Brief Introduction for Christians   *by Rabbi Eugene Korn, PhD*   5½ x 8½, 192 pp, Quality PB, 978-1-58023-318-7 **$14.99***

Jewish Holidays: A Brief Introduction for Christians   *by Rabbi Kerry M. Olitzky and Rabbi Daniel Judson*   5½ x 8½, 176 pp, Quality PB, 978-1-58023-302-6 **$16.99***

Jewish Ritual: A Brief Introduction for Christians
by Rabbi Kerry M. Olitzky and Rabbi Daniel Judson   5½ x 8½, 144 pp, Quality PB, 978-1-58023-210-4 **$14.99***

Jewish Spirituality: A Brief Introduction for Christians   *by Rabbi Lawrence Kushner*
5½ x 8½, 112 pp, Quality PB, 978-1-58023-150-3 **$12.95***

A Jewish Understanding of the New Testament   *by Rabbi Samuel Sandmel; New preface by Rabbi David Sandmel*   5½ x 8½, 368 pp, Quality PB, 978-1-59473-048-1 **$19.99***

Modern Jews Engage the New Testament: Enhancing Jewish Well-Being in a Christian Environment   *by Rabbi Michael J. Cook, PhD*   6 x 9, 416 pp, HC, 978-1-58023-313-2 **$29.99***

Talking about God: Exploring the Meaning of Religious Life with Kierkegaard, Buber, Tillich and Heschel   *by Daniel F. Polish, PhD*   6 x 9, 160 pp, Quality PB, 978-1-59473-272-0 **$16.99**

We Jews and Jesus: Exploring Theological Differences for Mutual Understanding
by Rabbi Samuel Sandmel; New preface by Rabbi David Sandmel
6 x 9, 192 pp, Quality PB, 978-1-59473-208-9 **$16.99**

Who Are the *Real* Chosen People? The Meaning of Chosenness in Judaism, Christianity and Islam   *by Reuven Firestone, PhD*
6 x 9, 176 pp, Quality PB, 978-1-59473-290-4 **$16.99**; HC, 978-1-59473-248-5 **$21.99**

* A book from Jewish Lights, SkyLight Paths' sister imprint

About SKYLIGHT PATHS Publishing

SkyLight Paths Publishing is creating a place where people of different spiritual traditions come together for challenge and inspiration, a place where we can help each other understand the mystery that lies at the heart of our existence.

Through spirituality, our religious beliefs are increasingly becoming a part of our lives—rather than *apart* from our lives. While many of us may be more interested than ever in spiritual growth, we may be less firmly planted in traditional religion. Yet, we do want to deepen our relationship to the sacred, to learn from our own as well as from other faith traditions, and to practice in new ways.

SkyLight Paths sees both believers and seekers as a community that increasingly transcends traditional boundaries of religion and denomination—people wanting to learn from each other, *walking together, finding the way.*

For your information and convenience, at the back of this book we have provided a list of other SkyLight Paths books you might find interesting and useful. They cover the following subjects:

Buddhism / Zen	Global Spiritual	Monasticism
Catholicism	Perspectives	Mysticism
Children's Books	Gnosticism	Poetry
Christianity	Hinduism /	Prayer
Comparative	Vedanta	Religious Etiquette
Religion	Inspiration	Retirement
Current Events	Islam / Sufism	Spiritual Biography
Earth-Based	Judaism	Spiritual Direction
Spirituality	Kabbalah	Spirituality
Enneagram	Meditation	Women's Interest
	Midrash Fiction	Worship

Or phone, fax, mail or e-mail to: SKYLIGHT PATHS Publishing
Sunset Farm Offices, Route 4 • P.O. Box 237 • Woodstock, Vermont 05091
Tel: (802) 457-4000 • Fax: (802) 457-4004 • www.skylightpaths.com
Credit card orders: (800) 962-4544 (8:30AM–5:30PM EST Monday–Friday)
Generous discounts on quantity orders. SATISFACTION GUARANTEED. Prices subject to change.

For more information about each book,
visit our website at www.skylightpaths.com